AF379231

WAR TIME SKETCHES
Historical and Otherwise

by

Adelaide Stuart Dimitry

Past Historian, United Daughters of the Confederacy
Stonewall Jackson Chapter, New Orleans

THE CONFEDERATE
REPRINT COMPANY
☆　☆　☆　☆
WWW.CONFEDERATEREPRINT.COM

War Time Sketches: Historical and Otherwise
by Adelaide Stuart Dimitry

Originally Published in 1911
by Louisiana Printing Company Press
New Orleans, Louisiana

Reprint Edition © 2014
The Confederate Reprint Company
Post Office Box 2027
Toccoa, Georgia 30577
www.confederatereprint.com

Cover and Interior Design by
Magnolia Graphic Design
www.magnoliagraphicdesign.com

ISBN-13: 978-0692322109
ISBN-10: 0692322108

PREFACE

The following papers, written by Mrs. Dimitry while Historian of the "Stonewall Jackson Chapter" of New Orleans, were intended not solely to amuse and interest, but primarily to set forth in correct form historic events of the war of 1861-'65, and further to preserve and hand down to an interested posterity incidents semi-biographical which otherwise would have passed into oblivion.

The author has derived her data not alone from written history, but largely from the lips of those who were participants in that memorable struggle – men who had been comrades of Mumford, confreres of Benjamin, and survivors of the ill-fated *Louisiana*. Material for the sketches of social life were drawn from the reminiscences of war-time women, mostly members of the Chapter, and all are based upon incidents occurring in real life. They shed side-lights upon the manners, customs and dress of that troublous period and reflect in their shining depths the high courage and quick wit of the women of the South-land.

As a woman of the sixties Mrs. Dimitry herself writes in *propria persona* for she was one of the signers of those "fair Confederate bank notes," serving the Confederate government until its downfall. Born of splendid Southern lineage, a Mississippian, but of the Stuart family of Virginia and cousin to that chevalier Stuart "*sans peur and sans reproche,*" she was qualified both by birth and experience to write feelingly and in authentic fashion. As the wife and intellectual helpmate of Prof. John Dimitry, she lived in an atmosphere of culture and scholarship.

Professor Dimitry came of a family of educators and literary folk and was himself an historian of considerable merit, notable among his works being a *School History and Geography of Louisiana* and *The Confederate Military History of Louisiana*. In this connection we can not refrain from quoting his peerless epitaph to Albert Sidney Johnston, engraved in the tomb of the Army of Tennessee, Metairie Cemetery, New Orleans. In its epigrammatic terseness of phrase, beauty of diction and poetic depth of feeling it deserves to rank as a classic.

Behind this Stone is laid,
For a Season,
ALBERT SIDNEY JOHNSTON
A General in the Army of the Confederate States,
Who fell at Shiloh, Tennessee,
On the sixth day of April, A.D.,
Eighteen hundred and sixty-two.
A man tried in many high offices
And critical Enterprises,
And found faithful in all;
His life was one long Sacrifice of Interest to
Conscience;
And even that life, on a woeful Sabbath,

Did he yield as a Holocaust at his Country's Need.
Not wholly understood was he while he lived;
But, in his death, his Greatness stands confess'd
In a People's tears.
Resolute, moderate, clear of envy, yet not wanting
In that finer Ambition, which makes men great and
pure;
In his Honor – impregnable;
In his Simplicity – sublime;
No Country e'er had a truer Son – no Cause a nobler
Champion;
No People a bolder Defender – no Principle a purer
Victim,
Than the dead Soldier
Who sleeps here!
The Cause for which he perished is lost –
The People for whom he fought are crush'd –
The Hopes in which he trusted are shatter'd –
The Flag he loved guides no more the charging lines;
But his Fame, consigned to the keeping of that Time,
which,
Happily, is not so much the Tomb of Virtue as its
Shrine,
Shall, in the years to come, fire Modest Worth to
Noble Ends.
In honor, now, our great Captain rests;
A bereaved People mourn him;
Three Commonwealths proudly claim him;
And History shall cherish him
Among those Choicer Spirits, who, holding their
Conscience unmix'd with blame,
Have been, in all Conjectures, true to themselves, their
People, and their God.

Realizing as loyal Daughters of the Confederacy that a true and absolutely unbiased history of the war between the States has yet to be written and that ours is the task of insisting on the truth of history as taught and of helping collect and preserve historic data, much of which is fast passing into oblivion with the ever-thinning ranks of the gray, this Chapter has accordingly striven to make the historic a salient feature of its work. As Daughter and Historian Mrs. Dimitry was ever faithful to her trust, and in her tender yet impartial way has embalmed sweet memories in our hearts and written herself down among those choicer spirits who "have been, in all conjunctures, true to themselves, their people and their God."

M. G. H.

CONTENTS

☆　☆　☆　☆

PART I

CHAPTER ONE
The Battle of the Handkerchiefs 11

CHAPTER TWO
William B. Mumford 19

CHAPTER THREE
The Queen of the Mississippi 25

CHAPTER FOUR
Memminger's Canaries 33

CHAPTER FIVE
Judah P. Benjamin 39

CHAPTER SIX
The Louisiana 49

CHAPTER SEVEN
Four Richmond Girls 57

CHAPTER EIGHT
The Halt 63

PART II

CHAPTER NINE

The Confederate Girl (Part I) 71

CHAPTER TEN

The Confederate Girl (Part II) 79

CHAPTER ELEVEN

A True Story 87

CHAPTER TWELVE

Davidson's Raid 95

CHAPTER THIRTEEN

A Rambling Talk of Richmond 103

CHAPTER FOURTEEN

A Woman of the Sixties 109

CHAPTER FIFTEEN

A Confederate Hoop Skirt 117

CHAPTER SIXTEEN

Mrs. O'Flaherty's Funeral 127

CHAPTER SEVENTEEN

An Incident of the Reconstruction 133

CHAPTER EIGHTEEN

Freedom's Shriek 139

PART I

CHAPTER ONE

☆　☆　☆　☆

The Battle of the Handkerchiefs

In the early forenoon of February 20, 1863, a whisper ran through New Orleans that the Confederate soldiers in the city were to be taken that day aboard the *Empire Parish*, Capt. Caldwell commanding, and transported to Baton Rouge for an exchange of Union prisoners.

The whisper grew in volume until it reached the ears of the Confederate women of the city. At once, gentle and simple, old and young, matron and maid hurried to the levee to give the boys in gray a warm "God bless you and good-bye." One o'clock was the hour fixed for the departure of the prisoners, but long before the stroke of the hammer on its bell, the levee for many blocks was densely crowded with people – a number estimated by some at 20,000. No New Orleans woman who had a brother, husband or son on that prison boat could have been kept away. These loving and patriotic women – many of them wearing knots of red-white-and-red ribbon or rosettes of palmetto, or carrying magnificent bouquets of roses, camelias and violets – like the flow of an ocean tide, steadily poured through Canal Street on their way to the river front. They debouched, a living torrent, upon the levee in front of the *Empire Parish* – a boat around which guerilla guns had recently been quite busy. What a waving of handkerchiefs was there and glad cries, and wafting of kisses as the sight of a loved face was caught in the prisoner crowd on deck! In the throng on the levee, redeeming it from the epithet "mob" could be noted many ladies prominent in culture and social position. Among these were the poet "Xariffa," dear to all Louisiana hearts, Miss Kate Walker, the courageous young heroine of Confederate flag episode, and Mrs. D. R. Graham, then a young wife and mother.

At first, the crowd was orderly though emotional, as was to be expected. Soon, between the soldiers on the boat and some of the Federals on shore began a banter of wits as to what each might expect the next time they met. Some ladies also, who were adept in the use of the deaf and dumb lamguage, were using this form of wireless telegraphy in talking to their prisoner friends. Through the dumb spelling tossed off upon their fingers under the eye of the unwitting sentinel, they learned that the baskets and boxes of delicacies sent to the Confederate prisoners in the Foundry prison had fed the thievish Federal guards instead of the dear ones for whom intended. This unwelcome news made more pronounced the attitude of defiance gradually assumed by the crowd. A wave of restlessness was sweeping over it. Someone cheered for Jeff Davis. A dozen resonant voices joined in the cheer, and quickly followed with a "Hurrah for the Confederacy," or as a Northern writer puts it, "shouted other diabolical monstrosities." The feeling growing more tense every minute was too strained for safety, and sure to snap in twain. Listen to the narrative of a participator in much that occurred on this eventful occasion:

"I do not know who conceived the idea of going" (in order to be nearer the prisoners), "on the *Laurel Hill*, the large river steamer lying beside the *Empire Parish*. My companions and myself saw the move and followed the crowd on board. As the day advanced, the numbers grew so great that their demonstrations of love and respect nettled the Federals. It was an 'ovation to treason' as they were pleased to term it, and they peremptorily ordered us to 'leave the boat, go off the levee, disperse.' The women could see no treason in what they were doing – merely looking at their friends and waving a farewell to them – so they made no move to obey. And this was what started the trouble. An officer, presumably under orders from Captain Thomas, then in charge, gave the order to withdraw the plank and cut the *Laurel Hill* loose from its moorings. Jammed from stem to stern with brave and dauntless women, little children and nurses with babes in their arms, the boat, with stars and stripes flying from its jackstaff, drifted slowly far down the river to the Algiers side. We held our breath as we went off, for we were much startled to find ourselves running away from the *Empire Parish*, but we waved a brave good-bye with our handkerchiefs to those on shore and they could not be kept from waving to us.

"After passing beyond the city, we wondered if they were taking us to Fort Jackson to shut us up as prisoners of war. 'Many a good Confederate has groaned within its stony walls, why should we escape?' – we whispered to each other drearily – 'but at least it will be better than Ship Island.'

"During our enforced excursion down the river, we learned afterward the Federals had certain streets guarded and permitted no one to pass. Relatives of the unwilling passengers on the *Laurel Hill* were wild with fear for their loved ones, and tried to get to the levee, but the guards brutally turned them back."

While the *Laurel Hill* was drifting out of sight, on the levee the crisis had been reached. The Federal guards grew tired of the noisy but harmless demonstrations and arbitrarily ordered the women to "fall back, fall back, and stop waving their handkerchiefs." They talked to the winds. Above the rasping order of the guards was heard a laughing retort: "Can't do it. General Jackson is in the rear, and stands like a Stonewall." Again was the order repeated and still above the din of voices and confusion of the multitude came the same jeering response that was caught up by the crowd like the echo from a bugler's blast. In the bright sunshine and friendly river breeze, more briskly than ever, fluttered and waved the exasperating and much anathematized handkerchiefs. Finally, Gen. Banks being informed of the state of affairs, sent down the 26th Massachusetts Regiment to clear the levee.

With the hope of quelling the rising tumult, augmented by the arrival of the regiment, a cannon was brought out and trained upon the multitude, the soldiers not caring who were terrified or hurt. In the meantime, imagine the feelings of those Confederate prisoners on the boat, forced to witness the cruel act of cutting loose the *Laurel Hill* with its freight of five hundred women and children, and the cannon turned on the helpless crowd on the levee!

But Gen. Banks met more than he reckoned upon. His cannon neither killed nor drove the women away, for, according to a Union writer, they presented "an impenetrable wall of silks, flounces and graceless impudence." The excitement was at fever heat. The women now wrought to frenzy with heartache and nerves, would not budge an inch, would not drop a single handkerchief even though faced by the murderous cannon. The soldiers first threatened them with the bayonet, and afterwards actually charged upon them, driving every woman and child two squares from the levee. But

> Defiant, both of blow and threat,
> Their handkerchiefs still waved,

and the onset of the soldiers was unflinchingly met with the parasols and handkerchiefs of the women. Only one casualty was reported – that of a lady wounded in the hand by the thrust of a bayonet. After the fray the ground was covered with handkerchiefs and broken parasols. At last, the belligerent women, tired out but not subdued, went home to sleep in their beds. So much for the battle on the levee. Our narrator on the *Laurel Hill* resumes:

"I do not know how far down the river we were taken, but I do know we had nothing to eat. In the late afternoon the boat hands were marched into the cabin to eat their supper and, when they had finished and marched out again, we were told we could have the hard-tack and black coffee that was left. Some of us were too hungry to resist eating, but the majority took no notice of the invitation. Not one of the ladies showed fear or anxiety. If they felt either, they would not gratify the Federals that much. The bright and witty girls made things very amusing with their *repartee*, when a good humored officer came among us, but some there were that were surly, and the guards at the head of the gangway heard many a caustic aside expressive of contempt for Yankees and devotion to the Confederates. There was no white feather among them.

"Slowly we drifted on, and no one would tell us where the Captain was taking us. After we were prisoners for a few hours, the ladies in passing through the cabin would ring the bell to let our captors know we were hungry, but none took the gentle hint and soon the bell disappeared.

"That night about nine o'clock we were brought back to the city, and when we were near the landing and saw that it was indeed home, dear old New Orleans, we felt so happy that we broke out into singing 'The *Marseillaise*,' 'The Bonnie Blue Flag,' and all the Confederate songs we could think of – our own dear poet, 'Xariffa' leading the singing. This deeply angered our Federal captors. To punish us, they said we should not land, and proceeded to back out into midstream, where they anchored for the night. The next morning, after sunrise, we were brought to the levee again – a starving crowd and cold from the night air. They set us free, I suppose because they did not know what else to do with so many obstinate rebel women."

So ends the celebrated "Battle of the Handkerchiefs," courageously fought on the levee, February 20th, 1863, by the Confederate women of New Orleans.

Authorities Consulted

Daily True Delta, March 23, 1863.

Rightor's *History of New Orleans*.

Written data furnished by Mrs. David R. Graham –
a participator.

Mrs. W.J. Behan's *Confederate Scrap Book.*

Mrs. Simeon Toby's *Confederate Scrap Book.*

"The Battle of the Fair," a leaflet written for the benefit of the Orphan's Asylum and signed "Miranda."

CHAPTER TWO

☆　☆　☆　☆

William B. Mumford

On the 26th of April, 1862, a boat manned by a few marines under command of a lieutenant, put off from the war sloop *Pensacola* that was anchored in the harbor of New Orleans. It landed at the foot of Esplanade Avenue, and its occupants hurriedly marched to the Mint. Acting without orders from Flag Officer Farragut of the hostile fleet, then abreast the city, the marines under the direction of their officer, hoisted the Stars and Stripes over the building that had been in possession of the Confederate Government for more than a year. As unwise an act, in the frenzied state of the public mind, as was the precipitate conduct of our young men later on.

In the crowd that soon gathered watching the marines at their nefarious work were four young men – Canton, Burgess, Harper and William B. Mumford. These felt it impossible, at a word, to change allegiance from the government of their choice to one they had repudiated; and, certainly, to the citizens of New Orleans at that time, this over-bold United States flag was as much foreign as that of the two dominations, French and Spanish, which once wielded authority in the State. By what right was it there? New Orleans had not surrendered. Gazing at the hated symbol of oppression forced upon them as it challenged the Louisiana sunshine and daringly waved in the river breeze, and catching sight of blue uniforms, not quite the fashion in this State since January 26, 1861, there was a sudden blinding rush of blood to the head that upset the balance of reason. It was too much for the patriotic quartette. Madly dashing upstairs, the first to seize the unwelcome flag was young Harper, but Mumford was credited with dragging the hated ensign through the muck and mire of the city streets, soiling and tearing it into shreds. All four young men were involved in what we now construe as a most rash, but not criminal, act brought about by the excitement of the time. Three of them escaped, but Mumford was the scapegoat that bore the heavy penalty for all.

Three days after, on April 29th, New Orleans capitulated to Flag Officer Farragut. Through the glittering pageant of the military occupation of the city that followed, one resolve – that of the death of Mumford – was never lost sight of by the invaders. But it was his own unguarded, boastful speech relative to the flag that is said to have been the immediate cause of his arrest. He was at once confined in a room in the northeastern corner of the Customhouse, where subsequently his imprisonment was shared by two of our veterans, Capt. J. W. Gaines and Mr. Howard Zachary. To us of this day, it is a matter of surprise that after the commission of an act which could not fail to draw down upon him the hostility of the entering army, he should have remained in New Orleans. Probably, his family was the magnet that held him.

On April 29th, Gen. Butler now being in possession of the city, announced: "I find the city under dominion of a mob. They have insulted our flag – torn it down with indignity. This outrage will be punished in such manner as in my judgment will caution both the perpetrators and abettors of the act, so that they shall fear the stripes, if they do not reverence the stars of our banner."

If words convey purposes, Wm. B. Mumford was by them prejudged. By the finding of the Military Commission convened by Special Order No. 70, June 5, 1862, it was "ordered that he be executed on Saturday, June 7th, between the hours of 8 a.m. and 12 m., under the direction of the Provost Marshal of the New Orleans District."

Influential persons interceded in his behalf, and it is said that Mrs. Butler entreated that he might be spared. But the Man of Infamous Orders was inflexible and his threat of punishment was carried out.

There was a certain dramatic effect conceived by Gen. Butler, in having this military murder of his take place from a gibbet projecting from the peristyle of the Mint and erected below its flag-staff. There, under the now triumphant folds of the symbol of Northern authority he so detested, just forty days after his futile attempt to destroy it, the life of Wm. B Mumford was taken from him in the presence of a large body of the Federal soldiery. Both cavalry and infantry were placed around the inclosure to overawe the vast crowd of sympathetic witnesses to his martyrdom. Governor Moore in a speech at Opelousas a few days after the occurrence says: "Brought in full view of the scaffold, they offered him life on the condition that he would abjure his country and swear allegiance to the foe. He spurned the offer. Scorning to stain

his soul with such foul dishonor, he met his fate courageously." In a newspaper clipping of that time published
in the *War of the Rebellion,* with much other data on the
subject, we read: "He died as a patriot should die – with
great coolness and self-possession. An instant before he
passed into the presence of his Maker he was cool in his
demeanor and on his countenance could be found no
trace of the ordeal he was passing through." Delving in
these same impartial records for traces of one whose
name seems "writ in water," we find that his execution
was the basis of official correspondence ordered by President Davis, through Randolph, our Secretary of War, and
conducted by Gen. Lee with the Federal Generals,
Halleck and McLellan – all of which resulted so unsatis-
factorily that Robert Ould, Agent of Exchange, was instructed on January 17, 1863, by way of retaliation, to
refuse Federal officers release on parole. In the proclamation issued by President Davis, in which he declares Gen.
Butler to be a felon and an outlaw, one-half of it is given
to an analysis of the Mumford execution.

If devotion to his flag, whether as civilian or soldier, be the test of a citizen's character, then surely
Mumford, judged by this standard, stands high. Through
history the one who has passed such a test has ever been
ranked nobly by

> That mysterious after-time
> Which circles round the grave.

Almost a parallel case with that of Mumford was
the rending from its staff by Col. Ellsworth, of the
Confederate flag that waved over the Marshall House at
Alexandria, Virginia, and the trailing it in the dust of the

stairway. Jackson killed Ellsworth for its destruction and himself, in turn, was shot by one of Ellsworth's Zouaves. Here a friendly book tells us that in sympathetic admiration "a monument was proposed to the hero of Alexandria and a grateful people contributed towards the wants of his bereaved family."

With Mumford it was an instinctive love for what represented the sovereignty of the South, and an ardent dislike for the emblem of Northern invasion that incited his emotional act. But it was an act committed in a Confederate State, of which the city was a part, not yet surrendered to the Union of which she had declared herself "free and independent." He died on Louisiana soil as truly a martyr to his love for the Confederate flag as did Jackson who was shot down in his own home in Virginia. The one before the city was occupied, tore down the flag usurping that of his choice; the other avenged an insult to the Stars and Bars that floated over his own roof. Greater love cannot be shown for a principle than by giving one's life for its sake. Both men gave this proof but, of the two, poor Mumford's was the harder fate. Jackson passed in storm, but quickly, while Mumford, after weary days of imprisonment, met a felon's death.

It is a matter for surprise and regret that the first martyr to Butler's regime, whose shameful death stirred the entire Southern heart to anger, should be so entirely forgotten by the present. What token of remembrance or honor – save what is found in the official records of the war or a few scant lines in the telling of a military incident – has ever been awarded his memory? At least, we know where he sleeps. Sixty paces from the entrance to the Firemen's Cemetery on Metairie Ridge, he lies in a lonely, neglected grave, in the top row of the ghastly "*bovedas*," or ovens, in the inclosing left wall. The marble slab that shuts in his dust bears only the curt inscription:

Mumford's Grave

– his name even shorn of its legitimate initials!

Sam Davis, of Tennessee, died as a spy on the gallows, but his dual monument – the one in marble, the other in unforgetting hearts – effaces its shame and the Daughters. in honoring the gallant young patriot with their prodigal bounty of bloom, themselves are honored. Jackson's deed was in the same spirit as that of our Mumford – he is not forgotten by his fair countrywomen of Virginia – but William B. Mumford's name, with many, is unknown in the city he loved and in which he died, and, at least, the bold deed which cost him his life is held but a vague remembrance.

Both pitiful and strange, is it not?

Authorities Consulted

Rightor's *Standard History of New Orleans.*

Fortier's *History of Louisiana.*

Dimitry's *Military History of Louisiana.*

The War of the Rebellion, and others.

CHAPTER THREE

☆　☆　☆　☆

The Queen of the Mississippi

On the South's imperial river,
There's a name that fadeth never,
'Tis the name of battle's champion,
'Tis the peerless *Arkansas*.
For when navies all are rotten,
When the art of war's forgotten,
She shall lead the fleet of story,
Titled queen without a flaw.

In the fall of 1861, the Confederate Government ordered the construction of two gunboats by Captain John B. Shirley, at Memphis, Tennessee. Both vessels belonged to that formidable class of naval armament known as Rams. One of them, the *Arkansas*, was destined by its exploits to gain a reputation that will last as long as the name Confederacy itself.

After the capture of Island No. 10 by General Pope, April 7, 1862, the *Tennessee* – consort of the *Arkansas* – was destroyed to prevent its falling into the hands of the Federals, who were then making ready to swoop down upon Memphis. Ordered by the Government, the *Arkansas*, despite the unfinished condition of its hull, under the command of Captain Charles H. McBlair, was towed down the great river, up the Yazoo, until it reached the only Navy Yard in Mississippi. This primitive Yard – upon whose site now screams a prosaic saw-mill – was situated upon the east bank of the Yazoo, about the southern boundary of the small city of the same name. Soon it resounded with the clang of forge and metal, for brawny workmen wielding heavy hammers made their mighty strokes ring out in unison with the pulse of their own resolute, hopeful hearts. Lieutenant Isaac N. Brown, already with a distinguished record in the Confederate States Navy to his credit, was appointed supervisory workmaster for the completing and arming of the boat. The patriotic planters of Yazoo furnished laborers; forges were sent in; the hoisting engine of the steamboat *Capitol* was employed to drive drills. The logs that lined the inside were some forty or fifty feet long, hewed square to a dimension of one and a half to two feet thick. Her engines were taken from the Mississippi steamboat *Natchez*. The armor that plated her sides in rows of double thickness was of ordinary railroad iron collected from all over the State. At the bow, these iron plates were fashioned into a sharp point that meant murderous work when driven with force into the ribs of an enemy's vessel. One hundred feet in length, with a battery of ten big guns manned principally by detailed navy men, but with a sprinkling of landsmen in her crew of 200, and commanded by experienced officers from the old United States navy, she was, indeed, for those days, a formidable war ship. There were no curving lines of beauty about the *Arkansas*. Although the child of Confederate love and hope, it was an ugly, rough, sinister-looking craft that tumbled like an ungainly leviathan into the yellow waters of the Yazoo. The *Arkansas* was born of the need of the hour and was built not for grace, but for power and destruction.

From the fact that this famous gunboat was constructed of timber growing in the Valley forests when first the work began; completed at its navy yard through the patriotic zeal of the farmers and carpenters of the county and of laborers furnished by the planters, within five weeks after being brought up the Yazoo; with several pilots and part of her crew taken from the vicinity, it is only fair to call the historic ram a "Yazoo production."

It was due to Captain Brown's skill and intelligence that he was put in command of the *Arkansas* for its brief but glorious career of twenty days.

In the summer of 1862, after a day spent in organization and drill, Captain Brown started the Ram on her race of fifty miles for beleagured Vicksburg. That morning, the 15th of July, the sun rose in smiles and blessed her perilous cruise. Six miles from the mouth of the Yazoo river, Ellet's small fleet consisting of the iron-clad *Carondelet, Tyler* and *Queen of the West* kept steady watch. Instantly, so soon as met, like a shark running afoul a shoal of minnows, the *Arkansas* darted forward, steering directly for the *Tyler*. A running fight ensued. After chasing both the *Tyler* and *Queen of the West* into the Mississippi, she paid special attention to the *Carondelet*. A shot went so true to the vitals of the Federal boat with a stolen Southern name that she soon hauled down her colors; a few more brought out white flags at her ports and shortly after the *Carondelet* sank. But victory was not without loss to the *Arkansas*. Captain

Brown was knocked senseless for a time by a ball passing through the pilot house. Two pilots were killed. One was Shacklett, a Yazoo river pilot who, as they were carrying him below, had the courage and devotion to exclaim with his dying breath: "Keep her in the middle of the river."

Buoyed and borne on by the strong, friendly current of the Mississippi, the heroic *Arkansas* – although with smokestack riddled by shot and shell and pumping a heavy stream of water – stubbornly kept on her way. The great Federal fleet composed of Farragut's sea-fleet and Flag-officer Davis' river-fleet, like a forest of masts and smoke-stacks, barred her path. The *Arkansas* stopped not to ask the reason "why," but at once opened on the *Hartford* – afterwards the Admiral's fateful flagship at New Orleans, and soon all her guns were in action. Now began the real race, a race that was full of danger, a race through shot and shell, a race through bomb and mortar, a race through an entire fleet. The brave vessel was in one of the most desperate fights any one ship ever sustained since ships were made. In addition to the fire of the fleet, she encountered strange rains, and hails and showers from the Federal fortifications that lined either side of the river. There was no rest for the *Arkansas*. A target for a hundred guns, the heavy shot of the enemy pounded her armored sides like sledge-hammers. The day was still and heavy smoke-clouds hung so close that it was only through the momentary blaze of a discharged gun that aim could be taken. But never did the musical guns of Groningen more harmoniously sing their fierce *ut, re, mi, fa, sol, la* than did the guns of the crippled *Arkansas* make ready and joyous response to the enemy through the flashes of flame. Nothing could stop her! Onward through the fires of transports and vessels of war belching death, she boldly, unflinchingly fought her way.

Now, through the smoke and above the din of shot and shriek of shell, was heard a voice crying out that the colors of the *Arkansas* had been shot away. In an instant, a young hero, Midshipman Dabney M. Scales – with a courage equal to that of the wild, intrepid Beggars of the Sea – scrambled up the ladder and fearlessly treading the terrible path of death, swept by a hurricane of shot and shell, again raised the Stars and Bars aloft. Onwards, the irresistible "Queen of the Waters" swept her way victoriously – rushing through the deadly hail of iron hurled by two fleets of about forty vessels of war and emerging shattered, bleeding, weakened by heavy losses of her crew, but triumphant – to anchor safe under the protecting guns of Vicksburg.

On the hills above, Generals Van Dorn and Breckinridge with thousands of soldiers eagerly watched the brave race. All hearts were anxious and sympathetic, but the hands that longed to help were powerless to aid. The heroic vessel plunged through the waters firing in every direction, never refusing a challenge as each war ship in turn tried to sink or disable her. It was as though the bold heart of the Confederacy beat under her iron ribs! On she pressed, unswerving in the path to her goal, until, finally, as she entered her fair haven opposite the City Hall, with Southern colors still aloft, still streaming in the breeze, still gloriously defiant of the mighty men-of-war filling the river, a burst of enthusiastic cheering greeted her. It was an ovation to a conquering hero!

At night, Farragut's sea-going fleet and Davis' iron-clads passed down the river. They came by singly and, at their coming, the *Arkansas* – sorely crippled, yet ever ready for a fight – dashed out and gave each a broad-

side as it dropped past. Admiral Farragut, deeply morti-
fied at the success of the daring rebel ram in running the
fiery gauntlet of his two fleets, sent a last spiteful death-
dealing shot as his flagship went by and killed and wounded many of her crew. A few days later, her old enemy
Queen of the West, also the powerful iron-clad *Essex* under Captain D. D. Porter tried to ram or capture her. But
again the "Queen of the Waters" was triumphant. Both
ships were not only beaten off, but disabled. Captain Porter, "The Boastful," found the rebel gunboat more than a
match for his big *Essex*, and his next despatch to Washington must have been less rosy than usual. But now the
Arkansas, though lame and halt from her fierce fight and
with a crew reduced to seventeen, was called to another
field. She was born to fight, never to rest! Here came a
telegram from General Breckenridge in Louisiana to General Van Dorn invoking the aid of her guns, and forthwith
the *Arkansas* was sent – her blacksmiths making music
with their hammers on repairs as she laboriously steamed
down the river.

On the morning of the 5th of August, the attack
on Baton Rouge opened. All day long General
Breckinridge listened eagerly for the roar of the guns of
the *Arkansas*, but he was destined never to hear those
guns again. The last hour of the veteran ram had been
tolled by the battle-clock. Born in Mississippi, she was
destined to end her glorious career in Louisiana. Five
miles off, already within hearing of the artillery of the
Confederates, the engineer announced that her machinery
was so broken it could not be repaired. Alas! the old engines of the *Natchez* were no longer equal to the work
required. The heart of the *Arkansas* could no longer beat.
Sternly resolved that the foot of an enemy should never

tread her deck, with the deepest grief, her officers fired and left her. She was free to go where it pleased her – her guns all shotted – her colors waving in the breeze. One by one, those guns as the flames reached them, roared out; and so the last race of the *Arkansas* was run, not only without dishonor, but with a glory that will long be remembered on the shores of the great river.

And her Banner sparkled prouder
Till the fire had reached her powder;
In her loudest peal of thunder
Went the Queen of Battle down;
And in all her olden manner,
Flared her never-conquercd banner,
Sinking 'neath the Southern waters
That remember her renown.

CHAPTER FOUR

☆　☆　☆　☆

Memminger's Canaries

To the Secretary of the Confederate Treasury, Mr. C.G. Memminger, is accorded the honor of being the first official to avail himself of the talents of his country-women in the service of the State. In view of the fact that clerks of the Note-Signing Bureau were needed in the formation of a Government Battalion for the defence of Richmond, he decided upon the employment of ladies in that special bureau. There were nearly 300 clerks of whom more than half were ladies. In 1863, this division was removed from Richmond to Columbia, South Carolina.

A simple outfit – consisting of penholder and pen, a spring-clamp and a blotter-pad – was handed to the new employee and, by grace of her oath of allegiance to the young Confederacy, she was henceforth known in the small world of the Treasury building as a "Note-signer," or a "Bond-numberer." With a bundle of Treasury notes, eight to a sheet, flung over her arm, she then sought the desk allotted her among those who were, from 9 a.m. to

3 p.m., for long months to be her daily associates. It was a unique world of toil, for the toilers were those who, once tenderly reared in refinement and luxury, were now forced to earn their daily bread at a salary of $1,000 per annum, with such increase as might, from time to time, be allowed by Congress. No one was allowed to be a mere cipher filling up space, for the Secretary was something of a martinet and, during office hours, exacted strict attention to work.

No great amount of brain power was expended in signing one's name several thousand times in the course of a day; but, at first, the common quality of paper caused many pouts and some tears – a sharp pen point often jagging or blotting the note. Eventually, our Richmond mills removed the difficulty by their success in turning out a fair quality of linen paper so smooth of surface as to admit of rapid writing with freedom from blots and, consequently, less exasperation of nerves. Although forced to substitute lithographs for steel engravings on our notes, we thought they presented quite a handsome appearance, for it was Southern currency and our faith was unbounded that, "Six months after the ratification of a treaty of peace," it would be as "good as gold."

It was the special ambition of each lady to record her name upon that fair and costly note known as the $500. It was the highest denomination issued by this Government and had a noble beauty unlike all others. On the left side was our flag with its starry cross crowned with laurel; on the right, great "Stonewall Jackson," as the guardian of its honor, faced it with uncovered head. Although the writing of the signature was merely a mechanical process, the fact of being entrusted with the signing of a note so high in value always gave the recipient of this

coveted honor much prestige in the note-signing commu-
nity. As the notes were caught fast in one corner by
means of a clamp, signing a name eight times on a sheet
and throwing it over to take up another was swift work
that did not always admit of thorough drying. There was
an unwritten law to the effect – so it was whispered – that
the penalty for carelessness in blotting notes was redemp-
tion of their value out of the offender's salary. Shortly
after a certain lady's promotion to the $500 note, to her
unspeakable horror, a clerk placed upon her desk several
sheets condemned for blotted signatures, all requiring
duplication. For some days, the lady avoided the man-
ager's eye as he made his tour of the room, but pay-day
passed and she breathed more freely upon finding that her
salary was intact and the Government yet had need for
her pen.

What types of youthful Southern womanhood and
dignified matronly grace, of social position and heroic en-
deavor, were brought together within the dingy limits of
that old note-signer's room on Main Street – reached
only by a narrow stairway! The girls climbed the rickety
stairs, light-hearted, because filled with the joy of youth
– strengthened for the day's work, perchance, by a savory
breakfast of toasted cornmeal, coffee and baked sweet
potatoes. We had not yet reached the starvation days of
Richmond, when the hungry rats came out of their holes
and were fed from the hand, gentle and playful as kittens,
and there was murderous talk of turning them into broil-
ers for food. "Why," it was asked, "should Richmond be
more dainty than Vicksburg?" The girls of that period
were irrepressible and, on the calendar, every day was a
red letter day. They cried: "Glorious Lee and glorious
Jackson keep watch and ward, therefore, all must and will

end well." So they sang their rebel songs with unabated ardor, put white and red roses in their hair for defiance, and kept the hearts of their soldier friends aglow with their own enthusiastic patriotism.

But it was the Confederate matron who sorrowed ever, for she bore upon her heart the dual burden of anxiety at home and fear for the beloved ones in battle. On the faces of many of these most noble women were reflected the "divine lights and shadows" that tell of the soul's growth within its garment of flesh. So much of their time in the gray hours of morning was spent on bended knee, or in reading and pondering upon the bright promises of God! There was the source of that marvelous power which made their courage as invincible at home as that of the veteran on the field.

After the lapse of years, it is difficult to recall many, but a few names will give some idea of the personnel of the Bureau. Again they rise and flit, like eager ghosts, through the shadows of the past. There is Miss Darby, allied to the Prestons and Hamptons of South Carolina, passing many a jest in quiet undertones; vivacious Victoire Blanchard of Louisiana, in dainty *organdie* and silken wrap, with the voice of a lark in her fair young throat, keeps up a monologue in a charming medley of French and English; Miss Stuart, a pale, serious slip of a girl of the Virginia house of that name, bends over her desk intent only upon preserving the fair integrity of her name upon the $500 note; the ladies Garnett, Bartow and Norton, Huger and DeSaussure, of Cavalier and Huguenot ancestry, are placidly killing time by diligent work. Seated near is Mme. Proctor, the majestic sister of General Beauregard. What a picture she makes with her abundant snowy hair dressed *a la marquise*, clad in silk, in winter wrapped in velvet, and wearing the costliest lace. She is numbering bonds, but, with pen poised for a moment in air, in her erect regal dignity, looks not unlike Marie Antoinette when about to affix her signature to some royal document of grace. In those vanished days, as a queen, she daily gave audience at her desk. The younger ladies, with one accord when through with their personal allotment of notes, were ever ready to assist this superb old lady with her bonds.

Many of the note-signers of that year, 1863, dressed in most unusual fashion – a creation of hard times. Handsome clothes, that seemed sadly out of place, were not infrequently in that old room. But, while homespun was most durable, it could rarely be got; and though a simple calico dress was cheap at $30, it was cheaper still to wear the costly garments already paid for.

One day, in the yard, a pot of machine oil coming in contact with some burning waste, caught on fire. It seemed as if a conflagration was imminent. The smoke ascended and billowed through the room, causing a sad flutter and fright among "Memminger's Canary birds," as the ladies were facetiously called. They swayed from side to side peering through the dense clouds of smoke at the open windows, seeking an avenue of escape. Finally, moved by a common impulse, they rushed pell-mell down the stairs into the open street, some with hair flying in the wind, without bonnets, hats or cloaks – all forgotten in their mad panic. The worst that came of it was a waggish paragraph in the next day's paper.

There was one order of the Bureau officials, so considerate as to deserve mention. Whenever the day ended in rain, an omnibus was directed to stop at the door and convey to their respective homes, free of charge, such ladies as lived at a distance. This humane bit of courtesy, coupled with the rather humorous resolution passed by Congress declaring that in calling for the ages of clerks in various departments, it was not understood to include that of the ladies, certainly, in the eyes of the ladies themselves, distinguished our Southern Government as one rarely chivalrous.

The spring-time of 1864 with its lustrous mocking sunshine passed, and never were the *Solfaterre* roses sweeter, nor the oleanders whiter in the gardens of Columbia, nor the Congaree Falls more musical as we listened to their play in the midnight silence, and dreamed of Lee and victory. Then the long, slow summer came and went, and the dreary autumn followed. With its going, we began to live on anticipated horrors. The new year of 1865 dawned sadly enough. There was much talk of Sherman's advance, and an effort was made to draw troops from Lee for the defence of Columbia; but in vain, every soldier was needed for Richmond. After Sherman's burning of Columbia – involving the destruction of the money-printing machine and of a large amount of Treasury notes – there was some expectation at the close of February, of removing the employees to Lynchburg, Virginia, and of starting anew the manufacture of the notes. But chaos had come again and this scheme was never carried through. The collapse of all things dear to the Confederate heart was close at hand. Appomattox followed swiftly upon the evacuation of the Capital, and then "the Confederacy took its place in the graveyard of nations."

CHAPTER FIVE

Judah P. Benjamin

On August 6, 1811, in an isle of the Danish West Indies called St. Thomas, Judah P. Benjamin was born of well educated Hebrew-English parentage. This beautiful isle, as in sunshine and greenery it rests in the arms of old ocean, might well be called a Darling of the Deep. Cyclone and hurricane sometimes come to play rough games among its lofty hills; but usually no sky is softer than the blue dome above; no sunlight more bounteous in its floods of gold; no breezes more odorous than those which come from the salt sea perfumed by the richness of tropic bloom. And the cradlesong of the young Israelite born in the midst of this natural loveliness was the rustle of mighty groves of palms, mingled with the unceasing surge of the wild Caribbean Sea.

With such an environment of storm and grace, was it strange that our nursling of the tropics should, through all the years of life, have felt their quickening influence in heart and brain?

It is a coincidence that out of the West Indies should have come, from the twin-sister islets of St. Croix and St. Thomas, two of her greatest sons to unite their names and fortunes with the mighty Republic of the West. Alexander Hamilton came in an epoch of seething storm and revolution to be the trusted friend of Washington and to sit in her councils of State. Later, came Judah P. Benjamin to make himself ready for the services of a younger nation that the prophetic soul of Hamilton already saw dimly shaped in the future.

In 1818, the green hills of St. Thomas sloped below the horizon and the Southern Cross faded from view as – his fortunes at a low ebb – Benjamin *pere*, with wife and children, left forever behind the sunny little island to seek a home of larger possibilities in the United States. Landing in Charleston, South Carolina, he resolved to secure for his young tribe that liberal, lasting wealth of which adversity could not rob them. The children of Benjamin were at once sent to a popular academy. Here Judah proved so diligent and aspiring a student that at the age of fourteen he entered Yale. The soul of the ambitious boy must have grown dark when, for lack of funds at the end of his second year he was compelled to discontinue his collegiate course without gaining his coveted degree. Early realizing that he was no petted favorite of fortune, but that the glittering baubles of success and reputation were to be forced by his own unaided strength from her closed, unwilling hand, with the resolute patience of his race he at once faced the struggle.

In 1828, destiny drew the friendless boy to New Orleans. Here we find him in the office of a notary delving as clerk, but, meanwhile, scant as was his leisure, studying law and, the better to understand the complicated jurisprudence of Louisiana, mastering the French and Spanish languages.

At twenty-one, on December 16, 1832, he was admitted to the bar, and so encouraging was his future that, in the spring of the following year, with the confidence of youth in himself and in his own bright star, he led to the altar Miss Natalie St. Martin – a beautiful Creole girl of New Orleans. Upon her and the daughter Ninette, who came to bless their union, he lavished without stint all the wealth of his affections and purse. As he was now a man of family, he also became one of affairs. He spent much time on his plantation of *Bellechasse*, deeply interested in the chemistry of sugar, and gave his leisure to writing articles both practical and entertaining for magazines. Such work was delightful recreation for one who loved the humanities and was accomplished without neglect of Chitty and Blackstone. But while engaged in work so congenial the failure of a friend, for whom he had endorsed notes for a large amount, so crippled his fortune that he resolutely closed his ears to the enticements of literature, and turned with renewed ardor to the practice of his profession. Henceforth, though interested like a good citizen in all that made for the public welfare, the world knew him best as the silvery-tongued, eloquent orator, and famous, astute lawyer.

Elected in 1842, to the legislature of Louisiana, ten years later he was sent to the Senate of the United States. In that great body of statesmen he was peer of the highest. A disciple of Calhoun, he held to State sovereignty in his brilliant speeches upon noted questions involving the two great issues of the day – Centralization of Government and State Rights. Upon the secession of his adopted State, with warm enthusiasm of feeling and in far-reaching musical tones, he expressed his conviction that the "State of Louisiana had judged and acted wisely in this crisis of her destiny." His farewell address to his colleagues of the Senate, in its high-hearted, impassioned patriotism was declared by Sir Geo. C. Lewis – a cool-headed, discriminating Englishman present at its delivery – to "be better than what D'Israeli could have done."

At Montgomery, in the formation of a provisional Government for the young Confederacy, he was placed in the Cabinet as Attorney General – an office for which his great legal abilities supremely fitted him. In Richmond, upon re-organization of Government on a constitutional basis, he was made Secretary of War. With its stern, dry complexity of duties he was not familiar, as several disastrous events soon proved. Not relishing the caustic criticisms of the public upon his administration of the War Department, he resigned his portfolio; but in February, 1862, President Davis who delighted in honoring him, invited him to take a seat in the Cabinet as Secretary of State – which he retained to the end of the Confederate Government. To him, both by training and temperament, diplomacy was congenial. True, he failed in his unwearied efforts to secure recognition for our young nation by the great European Powers; but we may safely assume it was because the Star of Empire shone not upon the cradle of the Southern Confederacy. When the swords of great Lee, Stonewall Jackson and Stuart could not achieve our independence, surely Benjamin may be pardoned that he did not gain our admission into the family of nations.

When Richmond fell, Benjamin, true to his personal friend the President, with the other Cabinet officers, accompanied him to Danville. All the long, dreary way he was the life of the party. When the President went southwards he was still at his side; but, on arriving at Washington, Ga., finding that further resistance was reduced to "save himself who can," he assumed a disguise and made his way to the Florida coast. Again, after many hardships, a "forlorn and shipwrecked mariner" life threw him upon St. Thomas –- the isle of his birth. Thence, once more he set out to fight the battle of life in a foreign land – this time, he was middle-aged, a man of fifty-five. Landing in Liverpool, he hastened to London and took up the study of English law. In June, 1866, a year after planting foot on the soil of Great Britain, he was admitted to the English courts as barrister at law. Six years passed, and in 1872, he became Queen's Counselor and presently was so famous as to appear solely before the House of Lords and Privy Council.

A portrait of him in his Counselor's wig – his dark, intellectual Semitic face framed in stiff rows of white woolen curls - clearly shows in its triumphant smile the indomitable heart and persevering genius of his great race. In his Hebrew lexicon there was no such word as fail. Overthrown on one plane, he never lost heart, but was ready cheerily to challenge Fate to another wrestle – ever another, and again so long as life lasted!

In the early spring of 1883, failing health admonished him to lead a less strenuous life, and he resolved to give up his magnificent practice which now ensured him a fortune of 18,000 pounds in English money – the third he had made. Before his final retirement to Paris, leading members of the English bar bestowed upon him a most unusual honor. Desiring to take a collective farewell and to testify their high sense of the honor and integrity of his professional career, and of their desire for a continuance of their relations of personal friendship they tendered him a grand complimentary banquet June, 1883, in the Hall of the Inner Temple. Sir Henry James on this occasion, in allusion to his forensic ability, voiced the recognition of all present when he asked: "Who is the man, save this one, of whom it can be said that he held conspicuous leadership at the bar of two countries?"

He did not live long to enjoy his honors, for the seeds of death were already planted in his frame. With the well-merited plaudits of all England ringing in his ears, he crossed the Channel for the last time. A Hebrew, he never obtruded, nor endeavored to conceal the birth of which he was proud. He might well say that "the world was his home." A man of two nationalities – British and Confederate – he passed the short remainder of his days chiefly in Paris, in the beautiful home he had built for his wife and daughter in the *Avenue d'Jena*. Here, he died May 6, 1884. He now sleeps in the famed Cemetery of *Pere la Chaise*.

*   *   *   *

And now by way of epilogue, let us take up a most interesting question.

Is it not singular to find that this great man – who in a momentous epoch of the national history cast his fortune with the South, when doubtless he could have secured preferment at the North – should be so misjudged and accused by men of the present day? If, as has been alleged, he carried with him the great seal, he but took his own property; for unless surrendered to the victor, such it became with the collapse of the government. He thus saved it from desecration; and if he retained it during life there was then no organization which could receive this, no doubt the most sacred of his treasures; and even if there had been, he was under no obligation to part with it until he chose. If, as has been asserted, he donated it to British keeping, he but put it into the care of the world's most powerful and most reverent custodian. And after all, is it not fitting that the longest-lived of the English nations should guard this relic of the shortest-lived? – that the symbol of our glorious quadrennium should abide among the symbols of a millennium, and that the mighty mother of nations should possess this memorial of the noblest of her daughters?

If Benjamin left the South in the day of her overthrow, he did no more than a score of her generals did, and no more than Davis was trying to do. Glance at the prospect before him as he surveyed the future with the President at Washington. The Confederacy was dead. The Chief Executive and his official family were fugitives. If captured, they could look for nothing less than imprisonment – a merciless vengeance, possibly the hangman's cord from the hands of a party at the North, drunken and crazed with power and flushed with conquest over their sister-section. In addition to this sinister prospect, he knew that all the resources and power of the Confederacy had perished in its death struggle. What was there for him in Louisiana, what could he do to aid or comfort her in her vast humiliation? Nothing! With the vision of a seer, he must have seen the destiny that was to be hers – the judiciary of which she was once so proud subjected to the rule of the sword, even judges holding their place by sufferance. The dearest part of a man's country is ever said to be his own family and fireside. Benjamin's household gods yet remained and his allegiance as husband and father was due to them.

Look at the long list shining with the names of other eminent Confederates who, after the surrender, in that first dark hour of collapse and a noble despair sought other lands in which to hide the agony of their hearts, in which to live or, at least, to breathe until health and strength came back to their sick souls.

Let us single out a few.

See Robert Toombs – than whom never breathed a more rampant, defiant, devoted Southerner – yet he, chafing at defeat like an entrapped lion, remained abroad until 1867.

John Taylor Wood – the brother-in-law of the President and his *aide-de-camp* – when all was over, escaped to Cuba and subsequently lived in Halifax, Nova Scotia.

General Early, after riding like a paladin long and hard to attach himself to a Confederate force and continue the war, gave up the fruitless chase and became an exile for a time in Mexico and Canada.

General John B. Magruder – called "Prince John" on account of his lordly air – sought relief for his exasperation by enlisting in the army of Maximilian and remained with him until his downfall.

Our own loved Henry Watkins Allen, Governor of Louisiana and gallant officer in the Southern army – unable to stand the changed conditions brought on by the war – took himself with his broken heart to die in Mexico.

But why add to the list? Against not one of these heroic souls of the Confederacy has envy or detraction ever raised slanderous voice impugning their patriotism. Why then against Judah P. Benjamin? Would it not be ungenerous to ascribe this petty resentment of which he is the victim to the fact that he was a Jew and, therefore, heir to all the obloquy that Christian tongues have too often meted out to his race? But, rather does it not remind one of the antique Cato's criticism upon the breach between Caesar and Pompey? "The great misery has not come from their being enemies, but from their having been friends." The South, resentful that another should claim the service and prestige of one whom she considered her own son, questions his purity of motive. A weakness of humanity! When a bond of union has once existed, we are apt to take ill even the appearance of a transfer of affection.

Instead of looking coldly upon one who was ever true to his brethren of the Confederacy, rather should we hold in highest esteem this official of our short-lived Government who in a strange land won honor and dignities so notable. Those honors, by reflection, are ours. Though the Atlantic rolled between the country of his early and that of his later life, yet will the name and fame of Judah P. Benjamin – three times chosen to a seat in her Cabinet – ever be proudly and indissolubly associated with that of the Southern Confederacy.

CHAPTER SIX

☆　☆　☆　☆

The Louisiana

In April, 1862, when the bruit of a naval attack upon New Orleans by way of the Gulf, first began to fill the air, it created little more apprehension than an incredulous shrug of the shoulders, or a laugh that one could be so silly as to believe the canard. Did not Secretary Mallory believe that the invasion would come from above the city, not below the forts? Surely, he must know better than these idle rumor-makers! Serenely, therefore, in the afternoon after closing his store, the merchant would stroll to the foot of Canal street to enjoy the fresh breeze, and while watching the swollen river – its muddy waters creeping stealthily but steadily, night and day, to the top of the levee – would speculate with his friends upon the probable height of the June rise, when the Missouri would empty upon its current vast floods of thawed snow and ice. Crevasses that endangered the orange orchards and fields of growing sweet cane troubled his thrifty mind far more than D. G. Farragut, "Flag-officer western blockading squadron."

Though the times were full of war, the Crescent harbor presented a scene of prosperity well-pleasing to the eye of planter and factor. A number of foreign steamers stood in the harbor laden with heavy cargoes of cotton for their return trip across the Atlantic. Around others at the wharves was the cheery hum of contented labor. The red-shirted stevedores, with their iron hooks were toiling and tugging, to the measured rhythm of an old minstrel melody, at the hundreds of bales that crowded the levee to get them aboard before night-fall. Up and down the sheds and over the wharves – as though a flock of sheep had passed through and paid toll with their wool – were great bunches and shreds of the fleecy staple, and everywhere the white lint floated in the pleasant April air. Out in the harbor, too, was a staunch little fleet of thirteen vessels, bearing among others such martial names as the *Warrior*, *Defiance*, *Resolute* and the *Stonewall Jackson*. Some of these were "converted vessels" – that is, river steamers made shot-proof with cotton bulkheads and provided with iron prows to act as rams, and among these were a few tug-boats for pushing fire-rafts on the enemy, should an engagement ever take place. Yet on her "ways" at the ship-yard in the Jefferson suburb was the naval monster, *Mississippi* -- since said by two navies to have been the most formidable war vessel ever built. Although unfinished, she was fast nearing completion and it was expected that she would rival, or out-do, the dashing exploits of the *Virginia* in Hampton Roads. The *Manassas*, glorious name but ill of prophecy, was lying above Fort Jackson eager to try conclusions with Farragut's fleet, should the Admiral be so daring as to extend a challenge. But above all, the heart of the proud city placed its trust in the *Louisiana*. Surely, that was a name to be relied upon as a sponsor for the protection of New Orleans! This formidable ironclad was not much of a trim, nautical craft to please the eye, but it was thought to be a fearful menace to the insolent ship that might brave its guns.

Far down the river – thirty miles from its mouth on the western bank – was Fort Jackson, guardian of the Passes and the first outpost of defence. Named in honor of the Hero of New Orleans, it bristled with guns and was garrisoned by a goodly complement of soldiers. A few hundred yards above on the eastern bank, the older fort, St. Philip, well gunned and manned, stood sentinel, and more securely to obstruct the river against possible invasion of New Orleans, was a barrier of schooners lashed amidships and anchored across the stream between the forts.

So, upon this fatal 24th of April, 1862, New Orleans, cradled in war, was not to be scared. Trusting in the strength and loyalty of her forts and in the might of her steam rams – two bearing as talismans against shot and shell the names of Gulf States, and one with the name of a Northern rout – she believed herself invincible. Off in the Gulf, an invasion that threatened might seem alarming, but in the city no one was alarmed. The laugh, the song and the dance went merrily on with the gilded youth on General Lovell's staff and the dark-eyed girls of Creoledom. In the gardens, the red roses and scarlet lilies bloomed in the spring sunlight with ominous significance of color, but the Queen City of the South – trusting in her defences on river and land – serenely pursued the even tenor of her way.

The *Louisiana* was simply a huge vessel built upon a dry dock. In appearance, to one not versed in naval architecture – as its unwieldy bulk lay heavily upon the water – it was not unlike the sloping roof of a house with ridge cut off by a broad open inclosure that, in turn, was surrounded by a parapet. Through this inclosure, like a curious swarthy giant looking out upon the world, loomed its smoke-stack. It was propelled by four engines and was to have been mounted by sixteen guns and carry a crew of two hundred men.

General Duncan, commander of the two forts, harassed by the fire of Commodore Porter's mortar-boats, called upon Commodore Mitchell of the naval forces at New Orleans for the services of the *Louisiana*. Yet incomplete, unwillingly, she was ordered down. With machinists and mechanics at work on her propellers, on the 20th of April, under command of Captain Charles F. McIntosh, she was towed down the river – as brave men believed – to be the guardian angel of the river defence. Half a mile above St. Philip she was moored to the left bank. On the 22nd, as the bombardment increased in severity, General Duncan requested Commodore Mitchell to move the *Louisiana* farther down the river so that she might drive the mortar-schooners off. The Commodore declined, for the reason that the *Louisiana*'s machinery was not yet in working order; that the engineers hoped to have it in a day or two; that its top was unprotected, and if a shell dropped on it, it would pass through the bottom and inevitably sink the ship, etc., etc. It was the same old story so often told of our gun-boats – a state of unpreparedness when occasion demanded their services. General Duncan, naturally believing that the *Louisiana* was built for use and should take some risks, felt aggrieved at the Commodore's decision – although in its propriety he was supported by all his officers – and unfortunately, from this time, all cordiality between the forts and fleet ceased to exist.

At 3:30 a.m., on April 24th, suddenly, in the midst of the wild uproar on river and land, in the darkness of the night, fell the silence of the desert. The mortars were mute; the forts stopped their fire, and the only sound that broke the stillness was the rush of the Mississippi, as the mighty current of its yellow flood went swirling in the pitchy darkness to its watery bourne in the Gulf. Inside Fort Jackson, just as longingly as the besieged Ant-werpers in 1585 watched for Gianbelli's "hell-burners," or fireships, that were to destroy the bridge of Farnese across the Scheldt, so did Duncan and the brave St. Mary's Cannoneers watch throughout that woeful, mem-orable night, counting the hours in hopeless despair of aid from the fire-barges at New Orleans. Through someone's blunder, the fire-ships, that would have carried dismay and destruction into the enemy's fleet, were not sent down on the one night when they might have turned the dark fortunes of the hour.

The sinister quiet did not last long.

In one awful instant a wild glare lit up the scene. Then like the deafening detonation of a volcano with its myriad quakings, throbbings and blazings came a crash and a horrible din. Porter's mortar-boats reopened their bombardment, with a shriek and roar of bursting shells, grape, canister and shrapnel. Forts Jackson and St. Philip responded with fury, but little effect. "Oh for the fire-barges whose light would give us aim and accuracy!" groaned Duncan, in his desperation peering into the dark-ness with a wild hope that he might catch a gleam of their flaming torches. But his appeal was heard only by the night winds struggling with the dense smoke that, belching from the mortars, added to the gloom of the night.

Under cover of darkness and the fierce hail of the mortar-boats, Farragut's fleet like ill-omened ghosts – each vessel grimed with river-mud to make it more a part of the night – under a full pressure of steam made the historic passage of the forts. Each one in rushing past poured broadside after broadside of shot and shell in swift succession into the forts. Once past, safe and victorious from the perilous transit, they steamed slowly up the river to their appointed rendezvous at Quarantine Station, six miles above. The passage of the fleet was brief in point of time – less than two hours – but long in tension as human hearts beat.

There were presages enough of coming disaster; but still above the forts floated the Confederate flag inspiring valor. Unhappily, however, the colors while inspiring courage could not confirm loyalty. Mutiny broke out in the two forts and signals were exchanged between the mutineers. Perhaps here best may be emphasized a consolation for State pride. No native Louisianian was among the mutineers.

In the meantime, the iron-clad *Louisiana*, pulling and tugging at her moorings and longing like a fierce mastiff held in leash to get at the enemy, had fired only a few scattering shots from her guns. Owing to the position in which she had been made fast to the bank and to the incomplete condition of her interior, her guns could not be trained so effectively upon the enemy's advancing fleet as had been hoped. After the gallant work of the *Manassas* in her bold rush upon the *Hartford* and her subsequent disablement, the *Louisiana* received her officers and men aboard.

On the 27th negotiations for the surrender of the

forts were initiated by Commodore Porter, of the mortar-flotilla. On the 28th, disheartened by the mutiny of garrisons in the forts and the reported capture of New Orleans, the conditions were accepted by General Duncan. Soon after, the *Harriet Lane* with Commodore Porter and officers – a white flag at the fore – came opposite the forts to receive and sign the terms of capitulation. Negotiations were proceeding amicably on the *Harriet Lane*, when on the Mississippi – of late so rich in stately spectacles – appeared a portent as awful as it was mysterious, floating by to interrupt the proceedings on board.

It was the *Louisiana*, once a powerful iron-clad, but at this moment a helpless wreck, drifting and discharging her guns at random. How worse than useless! The fleet which she had been specially armed to resist and terrify, was lying at victorious peace in the river in front of New Orleans. The mortar-schooners which she might, if properly handled, have gripped hard and sunk with her powerful battery, were near the head of the Passes, warily watching her and the forts. Hopeless to save her from the superior power bearing down on her from every side, her officers set her on fire, and sent her with all her guns protruding, down the river. Although in her death throes drifting aimlessly as the current bore her, she was more fortunate than her sister-craft – the great steam-ram *Mississippi* – which was taken above the city, riddled and burned before she had fired a gun! Abandoned to her own terrible self, the luckless *Louisiana* floated down in the presence of the guns of the mortar-fleet. The clumsy mortars, as she drifted past, struggled to escape the blazing wreck, even in its ruin a menace. When near her old moorings close to St. Philip, suddenly, from the great iron-clad came the deafening explosion of her powder magazine, scattering fragments of her wood-work everywhere within and around the fortifications; then a mighty plunge like some wallowing monster of the deep and the *Louisiana* sank into the abyss of waters! The blowing-up, as if in angry protest against surrender, shook the signers of the capitulation from their seats and careened the *Harriet Lane* on her side. Once righted, her officers rushed on deck, but saw only the river flowing sullenly to the Gulf, while not a ripple upon the surface showed where the *Louisiana* had committed her awful suicide.

It looked like the grimmest irony or a hostile fate, that the only casualties from the *Louisiana*'s formidable battery should have comprised one of our own men killed in the fort, and three or four wounded.

So, in a flame of fire, ashes and glory perished the ill-starred *Louisiana*, on whose strength and the stout hearts beating within her iron ribs had rested so many fond hopes. She never fulfilled the purpose for which she was built; but who dares deny that her phantom flag will float over the river, from New Orleans to the Passes, so long as the Mississippi has memories!

CHAPTER SEVEN

☆　☆　☆　☆

Four Richmond Girls

It was the 2nd of April of that most disastrous year, 1865, that Miss X. attended morning worship in the old Monumental Church of Richmond, Va. A vague unrest born of premonition seemed to permeate the congregation as, dismissed by the rector, they slowly moved down the aisles to the central exit. At the doorway, as Miss X. stepped upon the marble vestibule, her arm was firmly seized by a friend in waiting and she was hurriedly drawn aside from the pressing crowd. In a low tone was whispered: "I am just from St. Pauls'. The President received a dispatch and left the church in haste. Gen. Ewell has ordered out the militia. It is said that Richmond is to be evacuated to-night. Come!" Ominous whisper that boded much! A look that spoke volumes was interchanged and the friends silently tried to make their way through the steadily increasing, questioning crowds on the sidewalks. Already the direful news was in the air, but its effects were stunning rather than demonstrative of either anger or grief. It seemed as if a mephitic vapor had fallen from midair and clogged the utterance of speech. People looked at each other and in some subtle way understood that all was over, that love, valor, sacrifice – not even Lee in whom they trusted – could do aught more for the proud Capital of the Confederacy. It was doomed! And yet the heavens smiled serenely fair! It seemed so strange to see that bright sunshine on the streets and the skies so blue, when the cold shadow of despair was creeping over human hearts.

The friends hurried home and packed a few necessaries in handbags. Now, their number augmented by two others, they hurried to the depot. It was about 4 p.m. and the platform was jammed with struggling humanity seeking entrance to a long train that was drawn up for departure, and impatiently signaling to be off. What was remarkable was the fact that there were no noisy protests when trunks were refused or tumbled off when surreptitiously put on – whatever came was stoically accepted. All was confusion of moment; but it was a confusion dominated by a sullen silence of disappointment and heart-break. No ticket agent was in sight. It was "save himself who can." After vain attempts to gain a foothold, even upon the open freight cars, the four friends returned to their home. All Richmond was now upon the streets. They passed groups blanched in face standing at street corners, or leaning over the gates of residences asking in troubled tones for the latest news from Lee – their alarm increased by belated orderlies who, carrying despatches, clattered by with whip and spur. It seemed impossible for the four young women to get out of the beleaguered city, and yet it was equally impossible for them to remain and face the invading army on the morrow. "What was to be done?" they despairingly asked one another. They knew that they were desperately hungry, for they had eaten nothing for hours – that was the first point. After a scant meal of corn bread and cold turnips left from dinner of the day before, again the *quartette* with anxious hearts footed the long weary way back to the depot. It was now about 8 p.m. and the aspect of the city had changed. In the semi-darkness, companies of cavalry, like phantom horsemen speaking to none, but stern and grim, thundered over the stony pavements; the gutters ran a river of strong drink and a rabble, both white and black, knelt upon the ground and leaning over the edge drank of its flow like swine, or filled buckets and bottles to take home. Knots of negroes gathered on the sidewalks and seemed dazed, as if they could not make out the turn of events. Like their masters, thcy too were under the spell that forbade utterance or emotion. Through this half-drunken, but almost mute crowd, the four friends reached the depot. A long line of cars was drawn up that in the uncertain light seemed to stretch a league into outer darkness, and promise accommodation for the constantly increasing mob of refugees. But again the girls found that expostulations, entreaties, prayers were only a waste of vital energy. However, deliverance was at hand. A rough, but sympathetic official standing near, wearied perchance with the feminine din, gruffly said: "Ladies, this is a Government train with no room for civilian passengers, but, if you will go, the only place is on top of the cars. Up that ladder at the end is where you have to go." The friends, in dismay, contemplated what was before them. A perpendicular climb of several yards and afterward should they survive the attempt, a ride through rain or shine on top of a car. Oh, shades of Southern ancestry and instincts of feminine reserve! But it was the time for action, not words. Miss X. was a young woman of decision and solved the problem. Out of that city she had to go for her two brothers lying in soldiers' graves had sworn that their sisters should never be within the enemy's lines. Bravely, she seized a round of the ladder and with strong pulls finally reached the sloping top. Amid hysterical encouragement to one another, friend followed friend, until the four were aboard, drawn up close together on what seemed a central plank, on top of a carriage that promised both peril and discomfort. The train lingered and from their point of vantage they looked with aching hearts upon the motley scene below, and thought with dread upon what the morrow was to bring forth. The car on which they perched was out in the open and they watched the rockets, signaling retreat and disaster, flashing high up among the stars. They shivered in the chill night air and drew closer together as a dull report following an explosion was heard, or the blaze of a house in flames lit up the darkness. Towards the morning hours the train pulled out on its long journey, and the last view of the heroic city by the James was framed in the smoke and flames of burning cotton and tobacco.

Away the train sped through desolate fields, but ever under a mocking blue sky. Not much chance or desire for conversation was there. Sometimes, an overhanging branch from a wayside tree made the ladies duck their heads to escape a stinging slap in the face, and the swinging of the cars on long unrepaired roads produced a giddiness as if tossed on the ocean waves.

At last, the long dreary day ended. That night, April 3rd, at 11 o'clock, Danville was reached and the free ride was over. Half asleep from exhaustion and fatigue, stiff from cramped muscles and faint from the fast of hours, Miss X. and her companions backed down the narrow upright ladder and stood upon the ground. Imagine the amazement of the adventurous damsels, when horrified friends informed them that they had made the journey from Richmond to Danville atop an ammunition train!

NOTE: This and the following sketch are compiled from the author's own personal experience while as Miss Ada Stuart she served the Confederate Government so loyally and faithfully.

CHAPTER EIGHT

☆　☆　☆　☆

The Halt

The spring of 1865, in Virginia, was one of the fairest ever given to earth. There was a thrill in the air, a lustre in the light, a joyous beauty all around that seemed strangely out of tune with the sorrowful drama-of-war played by man beneath the ever-smiling, unclouded sky. The gardens bloomed like a second Eden; undisturbed by human tragedy, the aspens danced lightly in the soft sun-shine, flinging their gossamer lace-like shadows over the green lawns; and every breeze that swept the cheek came laden with rich perfume from the forest jasmine. None looking upon this delicate beauty, enlivened by the glad song of minstrel birds, could ever dream that the men and women of the Old Dominion were, in reality, a band of mourners gathered at a Nation's deathbed. The little town of Danville seemed a place for the soft, rosy dreams of peace and security, not for fear and wailing, nor for the bugle call to meet danger, disaster and humiliation.

It was here that President Davis and his Cabinet halted for a few days after the flight from Richmond. The reopening of departments, the dash of mounted soldiery, of couriers coming and going gave quite a martial, lively air to the sleepy, country town. Refugees came crowding in from all over the State, for the dread of separation from loved ones by falling within the enemy's lines was upon all. We literally lived out of doors those last days of the Confederacy, for hearts were too restless and oppressed to remain within. Sitting on the front steps, the swift hoof-beats of a horseman galloping past would bring every one in a tumultuous rush to the gate to scan his face and read the message it bore of good or ill tidings. It was in the air that our troops in North Carolina would have to fall back to some more distant Southern point; but we were not dismayed, for we understood that it meant only a new line of defence where Johnson would form and fight again. Then came the President's stirring, hopeful proclamation that rang out in our ears like the notes of a clarion invoking renewed effort and devotion. We caught its indomitable spirit, for Appomattox had not yet been reached, and we likened our gloomy present to the dark days of Wallace and Bruce when they fought for Scotland's deliverance. Boldness and adventure won for the Scots, why not for the Confederates? Our hearts, like that of the President, were unconquered and unconquerable. So truly confident were we that the God of Battles was with us, despite the fact that we were overborne by numbers; driven from our Capital; our once victorious army sullenly falling back, still we cried: "God is in it all – as truly in the dreadful retreat from Petersburg as in the sun-glory of the first Manassas." Though fronting constant disaster, our hearts stubbornly assumed that victory, in the end, would crown the South. Sometimes, however, when we thought of Lee in whom we always trusted, now so far away; of his right arm, great Stonewall Jackson, forever still; of his left, Stuart, that "Flower of Cavaliers," under the sod, in spite of the effort to be brave and strong against such heavy odds, a shadowy fear crept out of the future and chilled our hearts.

It was in this epoch-making time that two young Government employees of the Richmond post office – Miss Selden and Miss X. found themselves in Danville, still attached to the fortunes of a fugitive Government; but without opportunity for giving it service. Until the routine was established calling for renewal of their duties, they were fortunate in finding friends who opened hospitable doors to them. Miss X. was taken in charge by the mother of "raiding Jeb. Stuart," whom the fair Virginians dubbed "The Knight of the Golden Spurs." To be thrown so intimately with this distinguished and stately old lady, and to hear from her own lips, told with a mother's eager warmth, delightful home gossipry of the bold leader of the famous Pamunkey expedition, was an incident that appealed most strongly to the hero-worshiping, enthusiastic temperament of this young girl. It came into her life like a bright flower found blooming under a gray, wintry sky.

Several restless days were spent in anticipation of a summons to duty – varied one beautiful Sunday morning by church services and a prayer for President Davis. How little we dreamed it was for the last time! Then the two friends were notified to hold themselves in readiness to report to their department at Greensboro, North Carolina. The sunny afternoon upon which they received orders found them promptly at the depot. They were at once given accommodations in a rough box car whose sole merit was that it was wholly private to themselves. It was roomy, but with open doors, and void of any attempt at comfort or convenience. Its furniture was limited to two chairs and some nondescript luggage. The fearless temper of the women of that time is clearly shown in the fact that these two young girls – brought up in comfort and refinement, and with a most scrupulous observance of the proprieties of life – accepted the situation, not only without question or complaint, but with cheerful stoicism as a necessary outcome of the times. Alone in a box car, in a season of war; off on a train that went whizzing away to Greensboro like an uncanny monster in the darkness and silence of the night! A perilous trip for two young maidens, does it not seem – as we view it in the light of this quiet, uneventful prosaic present – forty-five years after occurrence? Life demanded prompt action in those stormy days and everything was so topsy-turvy that, if called upon to ride on the horns of the moon in discharge of their accepted duty, they would have responded to the call, feeling that some way would be provided to make the feat possible.

The train stopped a short time at Compay Shops beyond the Virginia line, and kind old Col. Clement of the Richmond post office, like a good Samaritan, sent a couple of hospital mattresses, a new tin basin and also some apples for the refreshment of the young marooners. Matters were much improved by his thoughtful kindness and in the twilight they became quite merry, as they spread their apples for a "starvation party" and speculated upon the future. President Davis and his aide, Col. Wm. Preston Johnston, loyal Judge Reagan with several other members of the Cabinet were in a car not far from that occupied by the two young girls. Judge of their surprise when a little after sunrise the next morning, Colonel Clement suddenly appeared from somewhere and asked to borrow the tin pan for the President's ablutions. Fortunately, their slight toilettes had been discreetly made in the early dawn so, regretting that they could not furnish towels also, the laughing damsels cheerily sent the pan for His Excellency's service and felt quite honored by the requisition – homely though it was. Later in the day, it crept out that the entire Presidential party, one by one, had followed their Chief's example in the use of the pan. Only an humble bit of tinware was it, but a relic to be sought after, when one recalls the distinguished and historic group of faces reflected from its shining surface.

From Greensboro, a day or two after, the Confederate Government as represented by its Executive and Cabinet went Southward. Then came the crash of doom! With the Government in the saddle, the two employee realized that the death warrant of all things Confederate was written, and their connection with the post office had ended without the formality of a dismissal. The "Lady Mayoress" of Greensboro, having heard of the freight car episode, cordially invited the young ladies to accept her hospitality during their enforced stay in the town – an invitation of which they gladly and gratefully hastened to avail themselves. In the meantime, events were making history fast. Fate struck the South two hard blows. One was the assassination of the Northern President, and the other – crushing us with anger, grief and humiliation – was the capture and disgraceful treatment of the Chief Magistrate of our beloved Confederacy.

The two young employees never understood why, or through whose agency they were awarded thirty Mexican dollars each, also a 20-pound box of tobacco apiece, as a share of the ex-Government spoils. What became of the tobacco was problematical, but the silver money came in most happily, for the treasury notes were now worthless, save for sentiment. On their return to Danville, Miss Selden finding the North an open door, at once went on to her friends in Maryland. Miss X. was again taken under the wing of Mrs. Stuart until, later on, she rejoined her friends in that city of ruins and sentinel chimney-stacks, the fire-scarred, blackened Capital of the dead Confederacy – sad Richmond-by-the-James.

PART II

CHAPTER NINE

☆　☆　☆　☆

The Confederate Girl (Part One)[1]

June 3, 1861: Tennessee severed her connection with the Union. At once "Soldier Serving Societies" were organized by the ladies of Memphis for the purpose of making uniforms and clothing for our troops, and the preparation of bandages, lint, etc., for the hospitals. Old and young, matron and maid were eager to aid in a cause that appealed strongly both to their affection and patriotism. Soon the gatherings outgrew private houses and, when other buildings were not available, the churches were pressed into service for their noble work – a work all untrained, but pursued with a heart and soul that gave it life and energy.

Among the numbers that daily crowded one of these churches – turned during the week into an immense sewing-room – might be noted a young school girl, Mar-

---

1. Data for this and the two following papers furnished by Mrs. George H. Tichenor, of New Orleans.

garet Thurman Drane by name, a golden haired lass of fourteen with eyes of Scottish blue. Ardently Confederate, each day after school she hastily tripped to church to aid in what warm fancy and a generous heart proclaimed a glorious task – that of making garments for the brave boys already on their way to Manassas, battle field of Virginia. Her eyes must have grown large from wonder and dim from dismay when the grey uniform coat of an officer was put into her untried hands to make. Poor little lass! She knew how to hemstitch, but not how to back-stitch, and it was before the days when sewing machines were made as much a part of the household equipment as beds and chairs. However, her heart was stout and with fingers both willing and diligent, after two days of hard toil and the breakage of a paper of needles, the coat was completed. Alas! when her labor of love was scrutinized at headquarters, no fault could be found with the stitches, but it was discovered that while the front and side pieces had been laboriously sewed together, the back had been innocently left out! She did not receive the blue ribbon for her work that day, but was assigned the less responsible task of bringing hot smoothing irons from the basement, upstairs, to be used in pressing seams.

A new hotel that had never been used as a hostelry was converted into a hospital and the city was divided into sections, each section taking its turn at service. The mothers, with a train of household servants nursed the wounded and sick, while the young girls carried flowers, wrote letters for the convalescent soldiers and sometimes – it was told with much glee by the mischievous recipients – they again washed faces that, in the course of a day, had already received due attention by earlier visitors, at least half a dozen times – all equally solicitous of giving aid and comfort to our brave defenders. Here came our lass – most eager to help, but so little knowing how. Timidly threading the long aisle of cots, she was implored by a soldier suffering from a gunshot wound to rub his arm with liniment to cool his fever and ease its throbbing pain. Proud to be called upon, her eyes bright and face aglow from sympathy, she seized a bottle nearby and hastily poured its contents on arm and in wound – bathing, saturating, rubbing it in with all the energy of which her young muscles were capable to make sure it would do good work. "Ah! unfortunate girl!" shrieked the soldier from the cot, his agonizing pain getting the better of his chivalry. At the sound of his wrathful voice there was a sudden flutter of skirts and patter of feet, for the young practitioner fled down the aisle that seemed endless, for fear that she had killed him! We will trust that the remedy was curative – it certainly was heroic and the pungent odors of turpentine were not a sweet, health-distilling fragrance in a ward filled with sick folk.

The days had now come when the looms of Dixie, hitherto an unknown quantity, were to be busy weaving homespun for its people to wear. But Margaret Drane with her sister and two young friends may claim to be the first of the "Homespun Girls" of Dixie of gentle birth who wore that much derided, homely material. A good-humored merchant of the city, doubtful of their brave, oft-repeated cry to "live and die for Dixie," resolved to test them on a point where he was confident their girlish vanity would shake their constancy. It was in the first days of the war when Southern maidens still affected what was dainty and becoming. Cynicus challenged them to put aside their pretty, airy, muslin frocks and walk down the fashionable thoroughfare of Main Street clad in humble homespun. While daring them to do this, he offered to make the material a gift. At once the quick pride of the Confederate girl was touched. She gloried in this opportunity for the sacrifice of personal vanity upon the altar of patriotism. The merchant's offer was accepted so soon as made and the girls marched in a bevy to his store. There they selected the unmistakably genuine article, with their own hands made the dresses in the style of the day -- ten widths to the skirt, tight waist and low-corded neck. Wearing their homespun, not as housemaids, but as if it were the ermine of royalty, and trying to keep step in their ungainly brogans; with cornshuck hats of their own braiding, bravely trimmed with red-white-and-red ribbons, shading their blushing faces, the appearance of the *quartette* on Main Street at once set the patriotic fashion and made them the toast of the hour.

Ah! those early days of a war that had not yet grown cruel and when, to the bounding heart of youth, the drama seemed just enough touched with danger to be wonderfully fascinating and entertaining! In the summer of '61 it was more of a game than a reality. Our girls, from daily visits to the soldiers' target practice, were fired with a spirit of emulation. "Who could tell," they reasoned, "but what, like the Maid of Saragossa, behind the rampart of cotton bales with which General Pillow has fortified the river front, we, too, may defend our city." True, many of the young maids had learned to handle without fear the pistols coaxed from brothers and friends and, too proud to betray ignorance, after a unique fashion of their own, loaded them. First they carefully rammed in a generous wad of paper, then bullets and all the powder the chambers would hold. But lo! nothing they could do would induce the weapon to go off and the entire contents persisted in rolling out. Again and again the charge was varied, bullets at bottom and paper on top, but of no avail. Possibly the cap was omitted. They could not tell, but cheerily looked to the future to remedy their inexperience and crown them with laurels. By no means discouraged, they turned to the target-practice, shooting with guns and cartridges already prepared and about which there could be no perplexing mixture of contents. Their spirits rose, for it seemed so easy. Margaret led her companions in this as in whatever enlisted the sympathies of her adventurous spirit. Ambitious to excel, she flouted the friendly counsel of her wise but over-mischievous escort, and chose for her first essay a sharp-shooter rifle intended to pick off its victim a mile distant. Averting her eyes, she resolutely pulled the trigger. What fatal ease! There was a terrific bang as if earth and heaven had collided. The rifle was dropped – our brave sharpshooter knew not where, for a space she knew nothing! Dazed by the shock of sound, she fell backward and rolled down hill to be picked up a somewhat bruised and aching young rebel, but irrepressible as ever and burning with the desire to fit herself for the service of Dixie.

If there was one delinquency more than another resolutely frowned upon, and that excited the keenest contempt of a Dixie girl, it was the cowardice of a man that kept him at home in a safe berth and left the fighting to be done by others. The girls looked upon that as a blot which all the power and wealth of the world could not purge away. Those not enrolled and known as "Minute men" – enlisted for the war and ready for the field at a moment's notice – received short shrift at the hands of these young fire-eaters. Margaret bribed a young man, whom she suspected of being unduly slow in entering the ranks, with a promise to mould the bullets he was to fire at the enemy. To do this tardy young Southerner justice it must be said that he was the only stay of his mother and she was both a widow and helpless invalid. But golden hair and eyes of Scottish blue have more than once taken the crook out of the way for a man. It was so in this case. The young man went to an early battle-field taking with him the pledged dozen bullets shining like newly minted dollars. Soon it was his good fortune to return proudly to dangle before Margaret's shining eyes an empty sleeve, and tell her that was her work. And the stouthearted little maiden was glad while she grieved, for the South's true boy had stood General Bragg's grim test of manhood – "To the front to die as a soldier."

So the memorable year of 1861 passed away and the shadows were fast deepening over the land. A typical girl of the '60's, our Margaret had sewed, wept and sung for the boys in gray through the golden summer months and early autumn days. At this time there was a Thespian temple in Memphis, newly built, but never opened to the player folk. The grand old "Mothers" of the city took possession of it and through local talent gave concerts for the purpose of equipping several companies with uniforms. Memory recalls one of those tuneful evenings, when all the girls who had melody in their voices gathered upon the stage arrayed in whitest muslin, with reddest roses for jewels, to sing the songs of Rebel-land under the waving Stars and Bars. And the rebel girls sang with a warmth and volume of voice that stirred tender old memories, or touched a patriotic chord whose vibrations set the audience wild with enthusiastic cheering and clapping of hands.

The *"Marsellaise,"* "When This Cruel War is

Over," then the sad sweet strains of "Lorena" in clear bird-like notes floated through the hall and a hush, born of its pathos, fell upon all. Who so deservedly proud as Margaret, our Confederate Girl, when one who loved the song told her that she sang it better than a great singer, claiming the fame of an artist! "Lorena" suggested tears and heart-break, so there was a quick transition to lively old favorites – as well known to the audience as the whistlings of their own mocking-bird – such as "Maryland, my Maryland," "Hard Times Come No More," "My Mary Ann," with a score of others, but always sliding at the close into the inevitable "Dixie" that was the signal for a shower of bouquets, sonorous hand-claps, pounding of feet, and strong-throated hurrahs.

In the meantime our Confederate Girl retires from the stage to come forth again with the story of her refugee life and subsequent return from Memphis.

CHAPTER TEN

☆　☆　☆　☆

The Confederate Girl (Part Two)

It was late in 1861 before Commodore Montgomery and Commodore Foote tried conclusions as to superiority of their gunboats under the bluffs of Memphis. Fathers of families, who by reasons of age, etc., were honorably exempt from military service and were at home, thought it prudent to remove to points less exposed to invasion by the common enemy. Margaret Thurman Drane's father – a minister who had figured prominently in the Alexander Campbell debates in Kentucky – decided upon Canton, Mississippi, as a retreat and thitherto our Margaret reluctantly went.

For the active, sunny temperament of our Confederate girl, Canton, a small inland town of Mississippi, proved rather a dull place of residence compared with the constant excitement of the river city, Memphis, in war times. The young girl's madcap energies must needs have a vent and with odd perversity reached their climax in the formation of a Cavalry Company. Among the numerous girls of the neighborhood she soon enlisted sufficient recruits, but, with all its rosebud beauty and grace, in picturesque accoutrements it might have vied with Falstaff's Ragged Regiment. A mixed multitude of mules and broken down army horses bore the joyous, adventurous patriots to the ground where they drilled by Hardee's Tactics. Their bridles were formed of bag ravelings and girths and blankets were made of gunny sacks. There were no privates in this well appointed company – it consisted wholly of officers, the lieutenants alone being seven in number! In her green riding habit Capt. Margaret gaily and fearlessly at the head of troop rode an army horse loaned for the occasion by a young officer at home on furlough. On a certain evening as she rounded a corner on returning from her daily drill, it so chanced that some soldiers were being put through military instruction in the taking of a battery. The drums beat, the trumpets gave forth a blare and the soldiers charged – yells of men and clatter of swords rising above the tumultuous dash and rush of horses. At once, Margaret's brave warrior-steed caught the familiar notes and needs must charge along with its army mates. No check of bit or bridle could change its course. Its mettle was up and the frightened girl, borne up the hill, was carried in the onward rush to the very front of the battery. Once there, having led the onset, the old battle horse halted, its ambition was satisfied; but the cavalrymen made the welkin ring with cheer after cheer for the dauntless courage and gallant ride of blushing Captain Margaret Drane.

Despite her strenuous, open-air life, our girl never lost sight of the practicalities. Confronted by the shoe problem – one that often tried the soul of a Dixie girl to the uttermost – in her own interest she bravely turned cobbler. From an old ministerial coat of her father's she cut out what was known as uppers. Carefully ripping the coat seams apart, she threaded her needle with the silk thus obtained for sewing on the soles, that meanwhile had been soaked in water to make them pliable for stitching. Tiny foldings of the satin lining made strings and lo! her small feet soon twinkled in new comfort and glory as, in pride and gayety of heart, she *pirouetted* from room to room.

Only six months of refugee life in Mississippi when the illness of a daughter left behind in Memphis called for the presence of one of the family. It was decided that Margaret should go to her. Fortunately, two old men, Messrs. Horton and King, the first well-known to her father, were about to make one of their periodical trips to Memphis. It was hinted that these old men were a brace of smugglers and spies but, as they were known to be on the right side in the war, loyal to the Confederacy and otherwise trustworthy, such small transgressions of the moral code counted for little in those wild days. Delighting in adventure and laughing at the perils of the trip in prospect, Margaret – confided to the care of these old men and with Miss Horton as companion – set forth in a topless buggy to make the distance between Canton and Memphis. It was just after Grierson's raid had desolated the land. The railroads were torn up, bridges burned and the long stretches of country highways were almost a continuous quagmire from the incessant rains. Seven days over these rough army roads, exposed to every whim of weather, brought them to Hernando, Mississippi. In the meantime Commodore Foote had taken Memphis after a most dramatic naval combat which, from its high bluffs, was witnessed by the citizens. Bragg was in Kentucky and Confederate spies were busy collecting and forwarding him information. The weather was sultry, but, despite the heat the girls had a quilting bee. They made, and wore beneath their hoop-skirts, petticoats, into which were stitched important papers to be delivered to agents in Memphis. Tape loops at the top of these petticoats made easy their quick removal should occasion call for it. Heavy yarn gloves of her own knitting covered Margaret's pretty hands, in the palms of which she concealed despatches so valuable that she was bidden to contrive their destruction rather than risk discovery.

After leaving Hernando and reaching Nonconnah – the little stream with melodious Indian name five miles out from Memphis – the girls took out their weapons. Bravely equipped with pistols they made the perilous crossing only to fall into the hands of a group of Yankee soldiery drawn up to guard the bank and fire upon all daring enough to come within range of their guns. They were at once halted by a Colonel – an elderly officer who threatened to have them searched at the barracks hard by. Margaret, having her head in the lion's mouth, was bent on saving it from being bitten off. Young in years, yet she was a true daughter of Eve and resolved upon showing a charming candor to this elderly man of war. Extending her gloved hands, palm downward to conceal the bulky despatches, and putting out her shapely feet encased in the cloth boots of her own manufacture, with a laughing look in her eyes of Scottish blue, she quickly retorted, "You had better search me when I go out of the city – that is if you can catch me. In our part of the world we have to wear shoes and gloves like these. And sir, you had better be careful for I have a Yankee sister in town." Her breezy air, perhaps the covert threat implied in her claim to Northern kindred, had the effect intended. The man of war was placated. Bending down, he whispered: "Little girl, I don't believe you have anything contraband. I like and trust you, and will take you at once to your sister's, and besides, I have a fine son you can marry." "Yes," replied saucy Margaret; "provided some good Johnny Reb doesn't shoot him." The daring girl felt the despatches burn in her hands like coals of fire. Outwardly brave, she practiced her coquettish tactics and the procession drove on, soon to pause in front of her sister's house. Eagerly she begged her escort to stop the horses a moment and, without pausing for his helping hand, so fearful was she that the wad of despatches might be detected, jumped to the ground and rushed into the house, Miss Horton following. Bewildered by her sudden flight, the deserted officer cried out, "You saucy little piece! I believe I'll have you searched anyhow, for now I think of it, I risk losing my stars if I don't."

By this time the parlor had been reached. The girls darted through the open door, in breathless haste locked it, then in a trice unlooping their quilted skirts with Bragg's precious despatches inside, rolled all up into a bundle and thrust it up the chimney – the open fire-place being concealed by a screen. No longer afraid of being searched, Margaret demurely opened the door and was engaged in quite a lively play of accusation and recrimination with the officer when her sister walked in to greet her. Being vouched for by one so high up in Yankee confidence was sufficient. The suspicious Colonel sloped colors and saluted. Henceforth the saucy little rebel was safe.

Margaret's sister and husband were both staunch Confederates but, through stress of circumstance, posed as friends of the Union. Consequently they were enabled to give much aid to the Southern cause. Mrs. Smith was permitted to visit the Horton House – converted by the Northern invaders into a prison for Confederates – for it was well known that she was a Southern woman who, despite her apparent Union proclivities, must have friends among the prisoners. On the present occasion word had come from Gen. Forrest requesting her aid in behalf of a certain member of his staff recently captured and confined in the Horton House.

Shortly after, Margaret was privileged to accompany her sister on one of her mysterious prison visits. Before leaving the house she was instructed to "do as I do." Mrs. Smith presented a pass from Col. Hillyer, the provost-marshal, permitting access to her "cousin," a young captain lately imprisoned. So soon as the guard called him forward she advanced cordially saluting him as "dear cousin" and apparently gave him a cousinly kiss. Margaret remembered her orders and did the same, adding in pity a warm embrace for a kinsman found in so pitiful a plight. "Oh, cousin, you look sick," exclaimed Mrs. Smith, whereupon the Captain staggered as if in severe pain, in tremulous tones announcing that he was "indeed ill, quite ill, but immensely glad to see her." Much mystified, Margaret listened to mutual recollections of a certain old Aunt Sally who made the best cornbread ever eaten, and who always made soup in her cabin and brought it in a broken pitcher to any one who was sick. This last feat of memory seemed particularly pleasing, but the captain's illness now increased so alarmingly that the sisters, after taking a much-concerned leave, hastily withdrew and the guard was summoned to assist him to his cot. The next day there was quite a stir and audible discontent in Mrs. Smith's kitchen. She insisted on compounding and herself baking a cornbread-pone, also pouring some of the family soup into a pitcher with a broken mouth. Bread and soup were arranged on a tray and carried to the prison by a servant, Margaret accompanying her armed with a pass to see her cousin. The Captain, still confined to his cot, was much pleased at sight of the food sent him, but the guard rather rudely called out that "it was queer eating for a sick man." Margaret explained that "he'd like it and get well because it was the same he used to eat at home." Soon she left her cousin to his homely repast.

The following afternoon, as six by the clock approached, Mrs. Smith proposed a walk in direction of the prison. On this eventful afternoon the sentry paced his usual distance in front of the prison walls. Margaret, while walking briskly and chatting in her own lively way, chanced to look upwards and so dreadful a sight met her eyes she gave a loud piercing scream. She saw a man dropping from one of the upper stories – falling to the ground, as she thought, to meet his death. A rough push from her sister, and an impatient order "to hush her noise" made her aware that she had done something amiss. The sentry in alarm drew near and to fix his attention upon herself she fainted dead away. Then, reviving, screamed with all the strength of her lungs and said she had fainted from a sprained ankle. The more the sentry tried to calm her the more unbearable was her pain and the tighter she clasped his knees. With lightning intuition she realized that it was a Confederate prisoner she had seen coming down his viewless stairway of wire, and that her sister was aiding in the escape of her pseudo cousin the captain. At whatever cost to herself the sentry must not be allowed to give an alarm.

Providence had worked his deliverance through the medium of a file baked and conveyed in the corn-bread, and a coil of wire concealed in the cracked pitcher of soup. After the war, Margaret learned that the prisoner was wholly a stranger to Mrs. Smith, but that Forrest had invoked her aid in freeing this member of his staff. She planned the method and means of his escape and gave the cues which he was quick-witted enough to recognize and follow to his deliverance.

CHAPTER ELEVEN

☆　☆　☆　☆

A True Story

On Sunday morning, August 21, 1864, Gen. Nathan B. Forrest, with about 1500 men in command, starting from Oxford, Miss., made his memorable raid upon Memphis, Tenn. For two days and nights his men were in the saddle, riding through blinding rains, in thick darkness, stumbling over roads heavy with mud, and swimming creeks swollen to the limit of their banks. They rode hard, scarcely pausing to eat their scant rations, with their wet, mud-clogged clothes clinging to and impeding their wearied bodies. At Hickhala creek and Coldwater river, it was necessary to build rude pontoon bridges lashed together with grape vines for cables, before it was possible for them to cross. But obstacles made the steel that struck out fire from the flint of this magnificent leader's nature, and from that of the iron-like men who rode with him. Light-hearted and gay as if going to a revel, they pushed on and, while it was yet dark, before the morning fairly broke, rode in silent, steady ranks into the city – taking it completely by surprise.

Once sure of possession the buglers, as if seized with sudden madness, broke loose, sounding the shrill charge and the men with yells and shouts dashed forward, clattering over the streets and filling the air with so outrageous an uproar it was enough to awake the dead. It woke the living who were asleep, and they sprang from their beds dazed, wondering if the foundations of the world had crumbled and the crash of doom had caught them. Some of the men under Capt. W. B. Forrest, a younger brother of the General, rode their horses into the rotunda of the Gayoso Hotel, in quick search for Generals Hulbert and Washburn. They hunted the building from basement to attic, but the birds were wary and had flown. From dawn until noon, Forrest and his men swept the city like a cyclone – only a bullet carrying death could stop them. Joy was in all the streets. At the corners stood groups frantically cheering and waving hats and handkerchiefs; leaning from windows hastily thrown up were women and children in night deshabille, who fluttered in joyous greeting whatever their hands first grasped, and made the air vocal with cries of welcome to the muddy but ever dear Johnny Rebs. One lady, an ardent Confederate, roused from her sick bed by the confusion and din, rushed upon the front gallery. On catching sight of the grand, erect figure of Gen. Forrest as he dashed by, she loosed from earth and trod the air! Clutching her two-day-old infant by the long clothes swathing its feet, she waved it triumphantly in the air as if it had been a scarf or a flag! After dominating Memphis so long as it pleased him – that is for several hours – Gen. Forrest and his troop leisurely rode off in the same direction whence they came, escorting a caravan of several hundred prisoners of war.

At the time of this raid there were living in Memphis a certain Mr. Smith and his wife – the latter, the lady who figured in the above incident of the baby. Circumstances had imposed upon them the necessity of taking the oath usually exacted of those remaining within the enemy's lines. But the observance of an oath taken under compulsion was rarely considered obligatory by the party compelled, in the lax days of the Civil War. Mr. Smith secretly bought and shipped ammunition, guns, etc., while his wife continually made purchases of small articles – medicines at different drug stores, tea, coffee, pins, needles, etc. – and smuggled them to friends in the Confederacy. Having quilted her purchases into a petticoat, she was ready for a ride. Her husband and herself were fearless on horseback and neither fence nor ditch could stop them. In the early morning or late evening they would canter down the main road leading out from Memphis in the direction of the little stream Nonconnah. Here the Federals kept a strict patrol and had a guard house – not only for safe-keeping such prisoners as they caught trying to enter the city, but also for searching ladies suspected of dealing in contraband of war. Mrs. Smith's horse had been trained at a given signal to run away. On arriving at the guard house, Mr. Smith would engage the officer in pleasant talk. Presently, his wife's horse becoming more and more restive, would suddenly dash forward, vault the fence and bear its rider away with the speed of the wind. The objective point was an old stump well known to the boys in gray. Reaching it, she would quickly dismount, remove from her thick coils of hair small packages of drugs, unloop her quilted skirt stored with good things and a correspondence that might not have passed muster at the city post office. Quickly concealing all within the stump, she would spring into the saddle and on her mad gallop homeward probably meet her husband and an anxious Federal officer coming in search of her.

Mrs. Smith's young sister, Margaret Drane, after six months' sojourn in Dixie, had returned to make her home for awhile in Memphis. A merry girl of sixteen with a piquant wit, she was intensely Confederate in her patriotism, and her dislike for the blue-coated gentry so frequently found in her sister's parlors was often marked by extreme frankness. Youth, laughing blue eyes and a frolicsome, even though pungent, tongue make a charm that condones all differences of opinion – so thought the Northern General John Morgan, the provost marshal Hillyer, and a score of other prominent Federals who greatly enjoyed provoking her spleen by narrations of Confederate disasters. They felt sure that the recital of these reverses would be sweet music in the ears of so good a Unionist as Mrs. Smith, and it was to them as nuts to a squirrel to tease the saucy, pretty little termagant.

The Federal officers in making their visits usually were entertained in the front parlor, while other callers assembled in the rear room. Young Margaret's voice was one of rare compass, strength and sweetness. Its exercise gave her a weapon which it was a keen delight to use against the military oppressors whose presence, though odious, she had to endure. She never refused to sing when asked, but gave, with unrepressed fervor, all of the Confederate songs she knew – and her repertoire was a rarely full one! "Maryland," and a version of "Dixie," more defiant than rhythmical, were special favorites for such an occasion and never omitted. One verse ran:

Dixie whipped old Yankee Doodle
Early in the morning,
And Yankee boys better look out
And take a timely warning.

One afternoon, Mr. Smith, in a low mysterious whisper for fear of listening servants, announced to his wife and Margaret that, through the connivance of their guard, he had obtained for eleven Confederate prisoners the privilege of visiting them at a late hour that evening. This guard, of course, had been heavily bribed both with money and champagne to allow them to leave the prison and remain out until 10:30 that night. Mr. Smith and the eleven prisoners gave their word that the return would be at the stipulated hour. So soon as darkness fell the prisoners came in escorted by their Yankee guard. In making ready for their reception, the shutters of the back parlor had been closed and thick damask curtains dropped to prevent even a glimmer of light from being caught on the outside, but to ensure safety, one window was left open and shielded by heavy drapery. In case of need, it would serve as an exit upon a narrow alley that ran between the house and a high board fence. This alley opened upon the street. All of these precautions taken, wine and cake – luxuries almost forgotten by a Southern soldier – were brought in to cheer both the inner and outer man. As friendly eyes looked into each other there was much quiet, serious talk in low tones – too low for Margaret, or the guard upon whom she was mischievously practicing her witcheries – to catch or understand. Thus pleasantly occupied, time sped for half an hour when, suddenly, the jangle of the door bell jarred the quiet. All rose and looked at each other in dismay. Mrs. Smith kept her composure, and with a warning to the young conspirator, Margaret, to "hold the fort," hastened to enquire into the interruption – a premonition of evil made her feel the presence of visitors before seeing them. On opening the door, behold, the Federal Gen. Morgan and his staff bent on passing a social evening!

In the meantime, all was quiet activity in the back parlor, the curtain was lifted from the open window and first the white-faced guard, then, one by one, the prisoners stealthily dropped into the alley below. Margaret's spirits rose to the occasion. At first echo of the bell, she had noiselessly turned the key in the door. The eleven men must get away and to cover their retreat – though her heart was going pit-a-pat for the boys in grey stealing off in the darkness – she lifted her voice in rollicking strains of "Jim Crow," "Dan Tucker" and all the noisy plantation songs she could recall. At each remonstrance from her sister in the hall as to her madcap conduct, she would break out into a higher, more jubilant stave and, with a chair for a partner dance a jig or a few capers of the Highland Fling – all to gain time.

Saucy, courageous, quick-witted Margaret! Her voice had the lilt of a mocking-bird and she executed variations, tremulos, spirited bravuras, extravaganzas of melody that would have won her encores on the stage. At last came the turn of No. 11. He slid out, let the curtain fall, then, crouching with his companions in the darkness of the alley, all waited for the hour of return to the hated prison. Our song-bird relished intensely this outwitting of the Yankee marplots in the hall. Continuing her bravuras and throwing a footstool across the room with a bang to increase the noise, she quickly gathered up the decanter and glasses used in their small banquet and pitched them out of the window – let us hope the crowns of her soldier guests escaped being cut or cracked. Then with a hop, skip and jump and a successful effort to obtain upper "C," she unlocked and threw open the door, her cheeks aflame from exertion, but full of dimpling smiles and arch courtesy of manner. In response to questioning from both sister and wondering Federal visitors as to why she had kept the door locked and created so fearful a racket, she merrily answered that her "old Johnny Reb sweetheart had come to see her, and she was so glad to see him it had turned her head."

If Gen. Morgan and his splendidly uniformed staff squinted at the sofa as they passed, to see if Johnny Reb was really there or had misgivings that something was below the surface, they gave no sign, but yielded to the fascinations of the charming young rebel, who, while brave, was never more so than in those moments of suspense when eleven lives trembled on the balance of discovery.

Had the guard been surprised in this escapade, death would have been the penalty as a soldier. True to their oath, the eleven prisoners were in their bunks at the prescribed hour.

A week later they escaped. It is not impossible to believe that the ways and means were planned on the night they ran the risk of capture, while a rebel girl sang herself hoarse to protect them.

*　　*　　*　　*

We take our leave of this true type of the Southern girl of the war period – high spirited, ever loyal, inventive, courageous. It may be of interest to know that our merry young heroine at sixteen was the bride of a gallant officer, who bore in his scarred body the certificate of honorable service, and that before the furling of our flag at Appomattox she cradled a young Confederate in her maternal arms and rejoiced that a man child was born into the world.

CHAPTER TWELVE

☆　☆　☆　☆

Davidson's Raid[1]

The pleasant little town of Greensburg, in St. Helena Parish, Louisiana, like Osyka, Clinton, and Camp Moore, was the scene of a series of Federal raids under Montgomery, Lee and Davidson, in the year 1864. Starting from Baton Rouge, they were planned, and fatally well executed, for the purpose of diverting attention from Sherman when he set out to cut the Confederacy in two, by his deadly march through Georgia to the sea.

The residence of the genial Sheriff, Mr. W. C --, was situated on a pleasant slope of green a mile out from Greensburg. Unfortunately it was in the line of advance of Davidson's raid. On a memorable day in November, just after the dinner hour of noon, the voice of the yard-boy, Henry, pitched to a sharp key from excitement and fear, was heard calling: "Marse Billy, the Yankees is coming!" Scarcely had the alarm been sounded than a regiment of

____

1. Data for this paper furnished by Mrs. J.R. Dicks.

blue-coated cavalry out on a raid came dashing up. A General Davidson, styling himself a Virginian, was in command – a small, wiry, dark-visaged man who looked as if he might hail from the Levant rather than from the genial mother of statesmen and presidents. One thousand strong the raiders filed into the entrance yard, or what was called the "Staump." This was inclosed by an old time worm fence, built with stake and rider – an inclosure that served as a barrier to the closer, more reserved yard around the comfortable mansion of two stories. With much tramping of hoofs, champing of bits, neighing and prancing, the troop of horse soldiers rode in, suspiciously alert for the whiz of a rebel bullet. The raid had for one of its objects the ferreting out and capturing of such Confederate soldiers as might be at home on furlough – so at any moment they might come across what they were seeking. The officers, quickly dismounting, tethered their beasts to the fence and issued sharp, rapid orders to the men for the night's bivouac.

At once, as lords of the Manor, they went to the cribs and helped themselves to the corn by armfuls, expeditiously shucking the ears and feeding their jaded horses. Then they scattered over the premises, a veritable swarm of locusts, seeking what they might devour.

In the meantime Henry was not idle. The creeks were dry, for the autumn rains had not yet set in to flush them. Into their many hollows, overgrown with the wild muscadine and grape, he hastily drove his master's horses. Unless they had gone down into the depths of the earth they could not have been more securely hidden. Here they subsisted on the vines and reedy herbage growing on the sides of the ravines so long as the raid lasted and the raiders were never the wiser.

Towards evening, General Davidson came to the house and demanded a private room for the surgeon of his regiment. He was suffering, so the General stated, from some acute disorder of his eyes and seclusion was necessary to his health and repose. His arrogant manner seemed to say: "Willy-nilly, he shall have it." There was but one room that could by any means be placed at his service, and that was already occupied by Miss Josephine R--, a young, flaxen-haired slip of a girl on a visit to the family. As General Davidson was so peremptory in his demand and had the brute power to enforce it, Mr. C. told him that it was impossible for him to eject a lady from her room for any man, sick or well; that Miss R's father was an Englishman and she had papers bearing the Consular seal to prove it. However, he would refer the matter to her for decision.

General Davidson was misled by the slight form that stood erect before him. Tall and slender, with a mass of pale gold hair, she was no Lydia Languish, but quite capable of proving her fiery Saxon and Norman descent. The Federal General renewed his command with the airy insolence of one with whom "might made right" and the girl before him was only a roseleaf to be blown away. His suspicious question: "If English what interest could she have in what concerned Americans only?" put her pride at once on the defensive. No "tranced summer calm" was hers. The color flamed into her fair cheeks and the silky, curving eve-lashes were lifted in haughty surprise. Clearly, but with a certain timbre of voice that denoted a danger spark, she informed the General that "her father was an Englishman from a family of no mean descent and she had the wit to appreciate the advantage and protection his English rights afforded her, but that, Southern born, she loved and was proud of the land of her birth. She was under the shield of the British flag and dared him to molest her. "

Upon hearing this from her own lips, the brave General temporized and putting aside his power to compel, made an appeal to her humane disposition in behalf of an unfortunate sufferer. "Indeed," exclaimed the irritated girl, "and where are you from and who are you that I should put myself out of my room to serve you?"

"General W. J. Davidson of Southern Virginia," was the somewhat hesitating response. Miss R.'s blue eyes flashed ominously. There was no culling of polite phrases, no mincing of words, but they rolled fast as if the fact burned her lips in telling it. "Then you are a renegade and I would not tell it. I am not interested either in you or your sick surgeon. Why should I be? In a war for Southern rights, you – claiming to be a Virginian – come down here and fight Louisianians on their own soil! No, I have no sympathy with such!"

This was rather a saucy bit of defiance on the part of a young Southern girl to an unscrupulous officer of the enemy, but it was the spirit born of the time. When a Federal aroused the resentment of a Dixie girl of the war days it broke out bright and scorching as the flash from gunpowder. The renegade Virginian dared not annoy one guarded by the British lion. He remembered that Butler had tried it in New Orleans but with ill success. Later, Miss R., deeming discretion the better part of valor, voluntarily surrendered her room and joined the family party of ladies and children in a more distant part of the house.

The officers of the regiment made headquarters of a large two-roomed building in the yard erected early in the war for the entertainment and comfort of passing Confederate soldiers. The rank and file made themselves happy for three days and two nights by using, like a band of roving gypsies, the fences around the cotton fields for their camp fires and in shooting pigs and fowls and stealing all the provisions they could lay hands on.

In those crucial days, Miss R. sat on the gallery, a Maid of Astolat, with the Richmond *Enquirer* for her magic mirror in which she saw the world go round. If one of the raiding officers approached her for conversation, she would regale him with accounts of the good thrashing Dick Taylor had given the Federals in North Louisiana, or news of Confederate victories in Virginia. With daring assurance she narrated all for their benefit with many a spicy comment.

Mr. C. had a valuable blooded horse which he was breaking into service from its freakish colt life. Expressing his anxiety about the safety of his animal to his young friend, Miss R., she laughingly told him to "lock Pompey in the smokehouse and give her the key. She'd take care of him." Poor Pompey found the change from his grass grown pastures and clear, sweet air to the odors of saltpetre and smoke and the carcasses of butchered swine to companion his solitude, too great for endurance. As the hours wore on, he grew restless and showed his disquiet by a continuous tramping and, in the semi-light, upsetting whatever he stumbled against. His performance had reached the climax when a little lieutenant – that, to use a homely word "piruted" everywhere, nosing into everything – passed the smokehouse and caught the sound of horses' hoofs exercising in a rather unusual stable.

Approaching Miss R., as she sat with eyes intent upon the *Enquirer*, he announced, as though fearing contradiction. "There's a horse in that smokehouse." " I shouldn't wonder," was her demure reply. "Then the door must be opened and I must have it. Get me the key," he ordered with military brusqueness. Miss R. was quite as laconic as he. "You can't get it," was all she said and turned the key over in her pocket to assure herself that it was really in her possession.

It is said that a gentle hand may lead an elephant with a hair, but we suspect that in this instance there was a more positive quality than gentleness which challenged the lieutenant's admiration. He looked at her keenly for a moment, and seeing that there was no quailing in the clear steady eyes lifted to his, dismissed further reference to the imprisoned Pompey and asked: "If I were to give you a horse, you little wasp, would you accept it?"

Miss R. was at once interested. "But you would only give me some broken-down barebones. Yet if you did, I would make it well and then give it to some good Confederate who had none. Try me," she saucily added. "Well you are a hornet as well as a wasp," was the nettled lieutenant's reply. "However, I'll be as good as my word. " When the Raiders once more took up the line of march he stopped long enough to call to a young darkey staring open-mouthed at the dashing cavalryman: "Hello, Sambo! you see that bay horse by the fence? Catch him and take him to the young lady on the gallery – the one with light hair – and tell her, because she was honest and brave the Yankee lieutenant sends it to her with his compliments. "

Before the last trooper disappeared up the long country road, Miss R. was in the yard hovering around her unlooked-for acquisition. With her penknife she bled the half-foundered animal and then – think of the bravery of this Confederate girl, oh, dainty ladies of the present day! – with her own hands, aided by the cook, forced down its throat a drench of alum and cornmeal. The animal recovered its strength and good looks, but as that part of the country was in the hands of guerillas and raiders, the expected Johnny Reb did not receive the promised prize.

No captured Confederates repaid the raiders on Mr. C.'s plantation. After killing all the stock, emptying the corn-cribs and sweeping the place clean of provisions they withdrew, packing off sacks of potatoes and such plunder as their stall-fed horses could carry. General Davidson forced Mr. C. to guide his troop through the hostile region. Once assured of the safety of himself and command, he permitted him to return home.

CHAPTER THIRTEEN

☆　☆　☆　☆

A Rambling Talk of Richmond

About the Confederate Dead Letter Office in Richmond, Virginia, was an air of mystery that, to the young and impressionable girls employed therein, made it quite an interesting place, despite its gloomy appellation. There was none of the bustling activity of life as seen in the upper Bureau of the Department, but the work was carried on in sedate quiet, and unconsciously, with lowered tones of voice. As if to accentuate its mortuary atmosphere, a skeleton dangled from the wall opposite the entrance, and daily seemed to greet the incomer with a sardonic "Remember to die. " It was said to be a part of the gruesome furniture of a doctor's office left for safekeeping on the day he went forth to battle for his country. In that strange winter of 1864-65, Life cheerily hobnobbed with Death, so there was nothing incongruous in working under the shadow of his stern, forbidding effigy. Judge Reagan was the Postmaster General, but as he rarely favored the small, dark office with his kindly presence, its supervision was turned over to his assistant and representative. This dignified old gentleman was a renowned LL.D. of Georgetown, eminent for his classical attainments and grand, Olympian presence. He held genial sway over a limited corps, consisting of two young girls and a sad-eyed member of the Departmental Battalion who was liable for service in defence of the city any, and every, hour of the twenty-four. The work from 9 a.m. to 3 p.m. was simple – merely to open and inspect the contents of letters that, failing to reach their destination, had been stamped "Dead." But it must be confessed that, for youth, it was depressing constantly to be confronted by that sinister word.

To the erudite gentleman who graced the head of the table were referred all perplexing problems found in the mailbags, such as letters that seemed to indicate a treasonable correspondence between spies in the city and their Northern accomplices outside; or others written in cryptic characters of dead languages, or any of the Latin tongues -- it was all one to his polyglot mind.

Of the two employees who "cheese-tasted" the text of letters, one, a lady of strongly Semitic face, was reported to be not only a faultless singer of oratorios, but also a writer for the city press; the other, a slender, short-haired girl, was one whose grand-sires, it was said, shared the blood of Rupert of the Rhine.

On the table stood two large flat baskets. One was a receptacle for coin, bills, checks, stamps; to the second was allotted the miscellaneous findings, that were as varied as the world is wide. In this old charnel house of the heart and mind was a curious and pathetic assortment of wares that floated from channels all over the country, and even from across seas. While non-intercourse between North and South was a military fact enforced at point of the bayonet, the passport system made it a fiction and Richmond, through blockade-running, at intervals was still in touch with Paris and London, and not only letters, but the vanities of the fashion world sometimes crept in. At this far day, the contents of the baskets would prove of little interest, but two bits of flotsam always seem to separate from the general wreckage and stand apart when memory goes back to those days. One was the portrait of a young Creole officer inscribed in passionate French to one who was *"tres chere, chere tonjours";* the other was a tress of brown hair knotted with blue ribbon and inclosed in a fair, unwritten sheet of paper white as the soul of the donor. Though mute, doubtless it had a voice for one who knew its meaning.

And so, conning these elegies of the heart, the hours slipped away until at 3 p.m. the courtly Professor tapped his silver snuff-box and, watch in hand, announced: "Ladies, we will adjourn until tomorrow." Spirits rebounded when that storehouse of the dead was left behind and, emerging from its gloom once more shared the life and genial sunshine of the streets. There is a droll ring in the fact that these girls, in making their way over the pavements of the hilly city, kept a sharp lookout for such pins as might have fallen and been lost by the wayside. Those indispensable little adjuncts of a lady's toilette were rare and costly in the war days. The supply came from Nassau, brought in by the blockade-runners, and were sold at $40 a paper. Necessity made the girls of Dixie quite practical, so, whenever a pin showed itself in the sunlight, it was regarded as treasure-trove and quickly picked up.

Once at home came the dinner – where it came from was the daily surprise of life. Sometimes it consisted only of a large platter of newly-dug goobers or peanuts, boiled in salt water, but always sauced with a wondrous appetite – in that dour time never lacking in Richmond. Thrice-blessed was the household so lucky as to have a country friend. An angel of relief she came in with a basket of vegetables – generally mustard greens – in one hand, covered maybe with apple blossoms to take off its sordidness, and bending under the weight of a big jug of buttermilk. What luxury and feasting for the next few days! What visions of savory dumplings with the greens, to say nothing of a left-over for salad! But oh, the eternal, dried, black-eyed pea whether in porridge or soup, baked or boiled, ever the same villainous comestible that made one weary of going to the table! The only dish that equaled it in atrocity was the stir-about of fried liver and rice! But the day was marked with a white stone, when, in the gloomy autumn days, friends sent a bushel of hickory nuts, a few tart apples, or a quart or two of ripe persimmons. In these days of plenty, it is hard to realize what a gastronomic treat was afforded by that wild, rough fruit, but it was welcome change from "peas-hot and peas-cold," so the Richmond starvelings thought them delicious, gave thanks, and eating, cared not for an invitation to the Queen's table.

In that ever to be remembered year of 1865, in the warm, luminous mist of early March, the peach trees on Clay Street blossomed. The pink shower of bloom – so unusual for the season and so lovely, coming at a time when hearts were so heavy – was taken by the young and hopeful as an augury of good for our Cause. But alas! for all our stout hearts, the starvation diet began to let its fine work be traced in the pale cheek and deeply shadowed eyes and, for many, beauty had lost its joy. The Treasury notes had become of so little value that it was a common saying on the streets of Richmond that you went to market with your money in a basket, and brought back your purchases in your pocket-book. The real heroes and heroines of those days starved patiently, with dignity and courage. Only extortioners and speculators could buy butter at $20 per pound, chickens at $50 apiece, and flour at $1,000 a barrel. But whatever their privations, the Daughters of the South never wavered in their two-fold faith in God and Lee. They reasoned: "If the fortunes of war force our armies from Richmond, the farther South is still Dixie and we can suffer and fight until we conquer." As to Northern domination, or Southern surrender, none ever dreamed of the possibility of either.

The Confederate woman was a "praying woman" – else she could not have lived and endured so nobly. Bravely she wore her "Iron Cross," graven not by the artificer in metal, but fashioned by Sorrow; not on her breast, but deep in her heart where the eye of God alone rested upon it. No sword in hand, no laurel wreath, no classic negligee for her sculptured ideal. She was no Amazon, but a loving, modest woman. Upon a background of blood and death, she rises the vision of a gentle, yet steadfast, white angel brooding over the objects of her love, with eyes ever bent upon the pages of an open Bible. Holy pages! that made her the ministering angel she was, shining and moving like those above.

CHAPTER FOURTEEN

☆　☆　☆　☆

A Woman of the Sixties[1]

During the early part of May, 1863, in the city of New Orleans, an iron-clad oath, as it was called, was issued by General Butler which ordered that every man who had not already taken the oath to the Union should take this terrible oath, within ten or fifteen days or be sent to the Confederacy as a "registered enemy. " The oath was so preposterous, that no Southern person could take it without perjuring himself dreadfully. My husband had belonged to the Home Guards and could not. A party of about seventy persons, including my husband, myself and three small children, left New Orleans about May 20th on a schooner so crowded that there was hardly standing room. Instead of making the trip to Pascagoula in about two days, contrary winds made it six, and a severe storm came up which put us in great danger. We camped at Pascagoula a week or more, waiting for transportation to

---

1. Compiled from *Reminiscences* of Mrs. L.C. Arny.

Mobile. The place was crowded with refugees – a miserable lot indeed!

After reaching Mobile, we found the city overflowing with refugees and it was hard to get any kind of shelter. We secured a dilapidated old place, and two camp stools with two single mattresses we had used on the schooner comprised our stock of furniture. Of course we slept on the floor and I used to look back at our home we had left as a palace! My husband at once joined a battery in Mobile.

I found a friend here whom I had known in New Orleans, whose husband had been ordered to the front before he could make suitable arrangements for her. So I brought her to my own poor home where her babe, sixteen months old, sickened and died. There was no direct communication with my husband at his battery, so it was certainly the hand of God that brought him to us in our terrible dilemma. Through the Louisiana Relief Committee he secured the burial of the little dear. Some time after, my two youngest children were taken ill, and I felt I would raise heaven and earth to get away, fearing they, too, might die. I feared the military authorities might think my husband wanted to leave, so I went myself to see Colonel Denis, the Provost Marshal, and told him the children and myself were a great disadvantage to Mr. Arny, and that his anxiety for us might prevent his doing his full duty. Col. Denis was of New Orleans, and treated me with the greatest courtesy and promised me a pass through the lines. After waiting two weeks, I heard that the schooner to take me was at Pascagoula. My belongings were all arranged to leave, but it was very difficult to get word to my husband and I felt that I must see him, as it might be a final parting. I went to the wharf where the boat came from the battery to get their meat, and found one just leaving. I tied a card addressed to my husband to the leg of one of the beeves, which he received, and came right over and procured a wagon with an old negro driver to take me to Pascagoula. Upon reaching Pascagoula, it was only to find that the boat had just left two hours before for New Orleans. I felt dazed and did not know what to do. Finally, I told the driver to take me to an old hotel where I knew refugees had camped, for I was not afraid, and knew that I had bedding and enough food to last awhile. My dear children know to this day what a coward I am, but nothing counted then. It turned out there was one man alone in the house, and when I saw him, I knew I couldn't stay there. So I went on to dear Mrs. Dodson's house – a place that I feared was too expensive for me, but she received me like a daughter.

The battle of Chickamauga had recently been fought, and the mothers had obtained passes in New Orleans to go to their wounded and dying sons and husbands – many of whom were numbered with the dead before they reached them. I was received like a dear friend by all. Oh, what a strong bond of sympathy existed between all those poor women whose husbands were in the army! A number of ladies had come from all parts of the Confederacy to get a flag-of-truce schooner to New Orleans. What a strange set they were! One poor woman died two weeks after coming and was buried under the pine trees. I was with her the greater part of the time and when she breathed her last. The doctors said she died of consumption, but I knew it was of a broken heart.

How eagerly we ladies used to watch the lake for a boat! I felt something must be done, for although Mrs. Dodson took Confederate money which had dreadfully depreciated, for board, I found I would have to use my New Orleans money and must get away. There were fourteen ladies besides myself, who agreed to get an army wagon with oxen and go across the country to Pearl River, where they heard Confederates had been given transportation from that point to New Orleans. The party, however, broke up except two young ladies and myself and babies. The two young ladies were sisters and they were indeed treasures. Miss Lillie Besancon was a beautiful girl, sweet and unassuming, yet a tower of strength, and helped us through many trials. We left Pascagoula on Sunday morning, the early part of December, 1863, with a negro boy of nineteen for our driver and arrived at Pearl River the following Friday afternoon. It was a very long, dismal ride through the piney woods with no certain road. The only guide was where telegraph poles had formerly been, but at that time there was scarcely a vestige of them left. We were quite out of the track for some time, which our faithful driver tried to hide from us. We rode all day and well into the night, until we found a hut in which we could shelter and rest. Those we had met on the trip were ignorant, homeless women and children, until the last night before reaching Pearl River. We then fell in with a desperate set of men and two women. The men went to the wagon and tried to break open our trunks. We had three very large ones and my blankets, which were quite a fortune out there. We put in a dreadful night, for part of the men were drunk and very insulting; but in the morning the sober men, and I think the women too, with whom we had pleaded earnestly, let us go on. The next afternoon we reached Dr. Griffin's and Captain Christy, whose schooner we hoped to board for New Orleans, was a couple of miles farther on. When we had reached that point, the Captain told us he had taken some Confederate ladies on his schooner, but had to pay dearly for it and saw no way he could assist us. His family were about sitting down to supper and he asked us to join them; but, as he had seemed greatly annoyed at our coming, we declined his invitation and told him we had some provisions with us. He was quite indignant and said that he was a poor man, but was not used to having people object to sitting at his table. Of course, we joined them and oh, how much we wanted that supper! We had been living on cold food given us by Mrs. Dodson for nearly a week, and we fairly reveled in those warm dishes. After supper, the Captain said he would do what he could for us. He would provide an escort for the children and baggage; but the others must walk and leave the house about three o'clock in the morning, so that the authorities would not know of our going. There was a fisherman a couple of miles down the river, and he was in communication with the Yankees – so we must be discreet. We had a very rough trip across the lake to Fort Pike in a small over-laden boat. We were received very curtly by the officers in charge and put in the guard-house. Miss Besancon was very charming in a simple blue, barege sunbonnet that covered her brown curls, and quite subdued one of the men by her sweet lady-like courtesy. The superior officer at the fort happened to be the same who, some months previously, had his regiment quartered on her father's plantation. At that time all of the men of the family were in the army, and the place was at the mercy of the Yankee soldiery, who cut down their fine oak trees, stole their oranges and committed many depredations. Mrs. Besancon applied to the Colonel for protection. He told her she should not be molested further and she was not. While the regiment was on the place they often exchanged civilities; but when she agreed to let his Adjutant practice on her piano, her daughters were much disgusted and kept out of his way. It was this young man that now came down to us at the guard-house and made many apologies for our being in that place. He said the Colonel had gone away for the day and locked up his quarters, but he would make arrangements for us on a gunboat lying out in the stream. He went with us very soon and introduced us to the officers who were far from cordial. We afterwards found out that some of the women they had taken to New Orleans had been very abusive of them. The accommodations on the boat seemed very grand to us, and the dinner was luxurious and beautiful with silver and china. Miss Besancon made a real friend of Capt. Groves, who was in charge. We started the next day for New Orleans. On arriving two conveyances were provided for us with an officer in each to drive us to our destination. Capt. Groves went with us to the office where we had to take the oath and relieved us of much of the embarrassment attending the many questions asked and to which we were obliged to subscribe. He then went with us to the prison where the Confederates were detained on some pretext. Our confinement lasted only a few hours, but some who were there told us they had been kept a week or more.

My New Orleans friends received me with the greatest affection and wanted me to stop in their homes; but I tried as soon as possible to get our home and furniture which we had left, and take boarders. The city was very full of people for they had flowed in from all parts of the North. Business was good and money plentiful. I had trouble to get my furniture and could not get my house under any circumstances. Finally, I left New Orleans on a steamer for New York the last of February, 1864, and remained in Georgetown with relatives until the close of the war. The siege of Mobile – where I had left my husband – was in progress and, on one occasion, I did not hear from him for six months. I heard only the Northern accounts of the war and when I read of ten and twenty thousand being killed in battle, I thought it was only a question of time when those brave men would be wiped out. Oh, how very old I felt! and, but for my children, would very gladly have shared their privations.

I sailed from New York to New Orleans, about a week after the hanging of Mrs. Surratt, to meet my dear husband, who was paroled with an honorable discharge from the Confederate army. We commenced life over again, and the dear Lord spared him to celebrate our Golden Wedding.

CHAPTER FIFTEEN

A Confederate Hoop-Skirt

About seven o'clock on a clear pleasant morning in the early autumn of 1863, an odd group assembled in the front yard of Mrs. Smith's pretty cottage in Memphis, Tennessee. Our scene takes place opposite the Armory – then held by Northern invaders, but formerly used by the Confederates as a manufactory and depot for cartridges. Our young friend, Margaret Drane, a trifle more sedate than when we last held pleasant converse – her golden hair in a twist or half curl swinging to her waist – came down the stairs gently supporting a tall, serious-faced, elderly lady whose years must have counted half a century. Despite her thin, delicate features, her figure was rotund, on the scale certainly two hundred pounds. Apparently she needed aid, for in her naturally easy, gliding walk there was a certain queer little halting movement that recalled the slow steps of a minuet, such as in childhood's days a Virginia grandmother described as the dance tripped in stately measure by high-placed belles of

117

the Old Dominion. Recent typhoid had made pallid and torn from the features of this old gentlewoman all claims to physical beauty, but though her appearance was grotesque and every movement marred by that queer little halt, there was about her the dignity and repose of manner which marks the true lady and shows that her life is governed by a purpose. A fervent Baptist in belief, a veritable Dorcas in good works, an ardent lover of the Confederate Cause, her friends asserted that she was never known to laugh, rarely to smile. Under all skies and every circumstance, life to her was stern, hedged in always by the grim word, duty. Peradventure, had the kindly gods Eros and Hymen smiled upon her youth, like the devoted Mrs. Gordon, she would have held her place in the rear of every battle-field on which her soldier husband fought; but the fact that her father languished in a Northern prison and three stalwart brothers were members of that invincible troop known as Forrest's Cavalry, constantly exposed to the bullets of the enemy, made such harsh demands upon her affections as to forbid all smiles and words of levity.

Arriving in Memphis, a few days previous to the present narrative, Miss Lucy – as she was affectionately called by her numerous friends – upon passing the Federal lines was instantly arrested and subjected to a strict examination. Freed from this indignity, very nervous and much bedraggled, she at once sought Mr. and Mrs. Smith, her city friends. The object of her braving the perils of a visit to Federal-ridden Memphis was to procure medicines for a hospital and clothing for her brothers. They like the majority of Forrest's hard riders, were almost as bare as the wild Irish Kernes when they fought in the Netherland bogs.

For ten days, Sunday not excepted, our frail, sad-visaged heroine would go out into the by-streets and suburbs of the city with loyal friends to make her purchases at different stores, of drugs, only ten cents worth at a time from each, in order not to attract the attention of Northern spies. Six suits of underclothing, also two pairs of cavalry boots, in addition to socks, handkerchiefs, etc., were gradually laid in. All of this made a large quantity of goods to be transported from within to the outer lines, but there was no limit to the patriotic devotion of our heroine and desire to make warm her three brave, soldier-brothers.

When the eventful day drew near for her departure, all was quiet activity in Mrs. Smith's cottage. The preceding night no one slept, for all were merrily intent on outwitting the Federals and eagerly interested in making Miss Lucy ready for her journey. Between two strong petticoats were quilted a quantity of medicine and tobacco. That was easy, but when it came to secreting despatches from General Bragg and other officers in Kentucky sent to Mr. Smith for forwarding, the conference was long and much puzzled. After a night of wakefulness, an idea suggested itself to the inventive brain of Margaret. The hair of Miss Lucy had fallen out as a result of her illness, and she had brought it to Memphis with the intention of having it converted into a braid. Luckily, too much engrossed with her brothers' outfit, she had not given it a thought. Margaret deftly turned this tangle into a graceful "waterfall," just then introduced to the fashionable world. Its capacious interior was rammed full of what little money was left from shopping and with it went the precious despatches.

At daylight Miss Lucy's toilette began, and never was a queen more obsequiously served, though the ceremony was enlivened at intervals by smothered giggles which the youthful Margaret could not always choke off. Over a soft undergarment Mrs. Smith, the first lady-in-waiting, buttoned an under-waist thickly padded with calomel and quinine; then came the skirt quilted with tobacco and divers drugs; the cavalry boots were suspended by a stout string passed through the loops of the boots at top and securely tied round the waist; but the large hoop-skirt concealing all this "contraband of war" might justly be esteemed a triumph of home inventiveness and patient needle. Made of white domestic with casings into which reeds were slipped, it was as unyielding and stiff as the farthingale worn by English court ladies of three centuries agone. Over the hoop fell the voluminous breadths of the homespun dress, standing out with a starched precision that rivaled the jeweled satin robes of coquettish Elizabeth Tudor, when she coyly curtsied to the deferential homage of "sweet Robin." A home-made palm-leaf hat with a bright blue ribbon passing in saucy color over the top was knotted beneath her chin, thus converting the flat into a jaunty scoop that gave room for the ample waterfall, and afforded a welcome shade from the sun in her long ride beyond Memphis. At last, our heroine – not one of romance, but practical and plain – was ready for her perilous undertaking, as much of a guy as loving hearts and willing hands dared make her.

A Texas mustang had been purchased for the occasion – beautiful in long mane and flowing tail when it scoured its native plain as was ever a wild horse of the Ukraine. But now, of all ill-fed, gaunt, woeful beasts of burden, none in dolorous aspect could compare with this poor victim of empty corn-bins. But its very woefulness made it the more desirable. The Federals watching at the fords of Nonconnah stream were too sharp to allow a good horse to travel beyond the lines to supply the need of some scout of the pestilent Forrest. Moreover, the rider arrayed "a la Meg Merrilies" and mounted on so ill-looking an animal would be less liable to detention if called upon to halt. "Bones" – as the laughing Margaret dubbed him – was led around to the front and stood at the sidewalk, wearily but patiently awaiting the next cuff his hard fate had in store for him.

To prevent the vigilant Federals in Armory from suspecting that the rebels were up to some disloyalty, it was prudently decided that Miss Lucy should mount her horse outside the gate in full view of all passers by. It was indeed an ordeal for a refined woman, but of what is patriotism and love not capable? Poor Bones, waking from dreams of corn and oats, sniffed the chair that was brought out to aid in the ascent to his back. It was like climbing the hump of a camel for, beneath his saddle, raising it unusually high, had been arranged in neat layers one upon another, the six suits of underwear. All of these were kept in place by a thin blanket. It was odd, but despite Miss Lucy's many excellencies, she generally created a deal of quiet amusement for her friends. Now, after careful adjustment of her hoop-skirt, she attempted lightly to swing herself to the saddle. Bones made his protest against man's inhumanity by falling flat down and bringing her to the ground with him. Here was indeed a *contretemps*! All set to work to extricate Miss Lucy who, with the unyielding hoop caught on pommel of saddle, was unable to rise. Opposite, the Federals stopped their work of making ammunition and roared with hilarious laughter. The negro house servants gathered at the open windows and looked on in sympathetic dismay. As for Margaret, the comic pitifulness of rider and horse was too much for decorous composure. She discreetly slipped inside the gate and, behind screening fence and under the shade of trees, rolled on the grass in a convulsion of suppressed giggling. "My Gord! Dat chile sure is sick wid de colic!" cried the pitying cook.

But even the bubbling laughter of sweet sixteen exhausts itself in time. Fearful of wounding the sensibilities of Miss Lucy – to whom though eccentric she was sincerely attached – Margaret finally scrambled to her feet and cheering poor Bones with friendly words and caressing pats of her hand, induced him once more to stand up and receive his rider. Time was passing and the sun gave warning to be off. Beyond the clear waters of Nonconnah, Confederate scouts had made tryst with the adventurous lady and her much needed wares, and that tryst she must "bide."

Here on the scene now appeared Mrs. Smith riding a blooded roan – striking contrast to Bones – and accompanied by her husband for a morning ride. In passing, she merely glanced at the group around her door as if they had been so many strangers, but that glance was enough for a cue. Then away in brisk canter sped husband and wife for the "lines," where all suspected persons either coming in or going out of Memphis were taken to be searched. Margaret, as her sister rode off, hurriedly passed up to Miss Lucy a bottle of Mustang Liniment, charging her "to throw its contents into the face of the first Yankee daring enough to try and arrest her." Giving a pat to Bones and urging him to "be off" and "be good," she ran upstairs to hide the light-hearted laughter which respect for Miss Lucy forbade vent in her presence. That charitable, unsuspecting lady ascribed her emotion to tears over the risk she was taking, and rode off in happy ignorance of her mirth-provoking aspect. Bones, stolidly bearing his burden but with many a limp and halt, slowly stumbled along in the wake of Mrs. Smith.

Mr. and Mrs. Smith passed Miss Lucy on the road without even a nod of recognition, and reached the lines long before she was in sight of them. Here they were soon engaged in a merry interchange of wits with some of the Federal officers, whose good-will they were politic enough to cultivate for the sake of the Cause. As the comical figure of Miss Lucy hove in sight, Mrs. Smith with a ringing laugh cried to the commanding officer: "Do look at that Judy mounted on Rosinante! You surely are not going to arrest that crazy looking creature are you? Better let her pass, she certainly will kill the rebels with fright. I had her for a time in my house and am glad to be rid of her" – and she tapped her forehead significantly. "But goodbye, your pleasant official duties are calling you" – and with another gay laugh and wave of her hand in direction of the approaching "Judy," rode for home. Looking back, she saw that the officers, acting upon the hint that her wits were disordered, had allowed Miss Lucy to pass without question. Her being sponsored by one so high in Federal esteem as Mrs. Smith, doubtless had much to do with her not being searched.

Happily rid of Federal patrols and guards, Miss Lucy, not pinning faith to Emerson's dazzling "seraphim of destiny," but serenely trusting in Providence and, maybe, with a soft strain of an old hymn floating musically across her mind, without escort, but also without misgiving, began to cover the long weary miles to the constantly changing headquarters of the ever-flitting Forrest. Unlike those of General Pope, his really were "in the saddle," for rarely did two nights see him in the same place and the Federals were always finding him where they least wanted him! Fortunately, Bones as if conscious that he was working in a good cause, held bravely up until beyond the Federal lines, but once more in Dixie, joy and weakness combined got the better of his good-will. Again he stumbled and fell – this time by good luck on his knees. Miss Lucy, on whose thin ankles the boots had pounded a tattoo at every step, clambered to the ground. She peered eagerly around for her friends the scouts; but Bones' plodding gait had spoiled all hope of meeting them. Those busy men, like the shadows of evening, had quickly come and, the tryst unkept, had quietly gone. With the air of one accustomed to disappointment and without further waste of time, she threw her weary burden of boots and quilted skirt on the pommel of the saddle and, taking the bridle in hand, fearlessly walked the long country road at the side of uncomplaining Bones. Providence soon rewarded her trust, for she overtook a cavalry wagon en route to Forrest's flying headquarters. A lift was gallantly offered her by the honest Confederate wagoner and with cheerful readiness accepted. Of what had she to be afraid? Was she not in Dixie with guardians all around her?

Finally, without mishap or molestation she reached her journey's end – at some vanishing point between Oxford, Mississippi, and East Tennessee, the famous stamping ground of Forrest's cavalry. In the joy of relieving the necessities of her proud and delighted brothers, our gentle spinster forgot the risks and discomforts of her really perilous trip. An innocent pride was hers as, in person, she delivered her military dispatches to the great Cavalryman, and heard the care-ridden hospital surgeon gratefully call her small store of drugs a "perfect God-send. "

Bones, less martial than the fiery "horse without peer" that brought the "good news from Ghent," to whom the grateful burgesses of Aix voted their last bottle of wine, was content for his patient endurance of ills, to receive a good feed of oats. Let us hope – though chronicles are silent on the subject – his last days in Dixie were not without comfort and care and that with food he soon lost the grisly name by which we made his acquaintance.

*   *   *   *

One word more: The uplifting sadness of Miss Lucy Jones was prophetic of future loss. Only one brother survived the war, and her father laid down his life in a Northern prison.

CHAPTER SIXTEEN

☆　☆　☆　☆

Mrs. O'Flaherty's Funeral

In the days of General Washburn's occupation of Memphis, when General Nathan B. Forrest with his cavalry hovering on the outskirts of the city was ever a menace by day and a terror by night to the peace and repose of the Federal commander, the following incident took place which well illustrates the grotesque humor that sometimes played over the stern realities of the Civil War. In South Memphis, in the direction of Elmwood Cemetery, was a livery stable owned and operated by an Irishman by the name of O'Flaherty, a man of substance who doubtless argued, like many of his brother Hibernians, that being the lineal descendant of O'Flaherty, he was also the descendant of O'Somebody, who was also the son of another O'Somebody, who went back in unbroken succession to the blood of Irish Kings. With all his heart and soul he "went in for a rebillion," caring little whether in Memphis or Cork. Through him, actively aided by his wife, also a child of the Emerald Isle, a constant communication was kept up with Forrest, and few were the movements of the Federals in the city but what were reported to and often thwarted by this bold, alert leader of Confederate Cavalry.

O'Flaherty's wife was indeed a kindred spirit, a spouse well chosen by an eccentric Irishman whose political creed embraced but two articles – the wearing of the "green above the red" and the "cracking of crowns." Having embraced the Southern side in the war between the sections, Dame O'Flaherty threw into the struggle all the wit, force and energy of a warm Celtic heart and mind ever bubbling over with humorous subtlety.

No half measures would do for her. She learned that Forrest's brave men were sadly in need of guns, ammunition and supplies of clothing. To hear of their sorrowful plight was an irresistible appeal to her newly adopted patriotism. She resolved that what they wanted they should have and straight-way sat plotting for the ways and means. "Why," she soliloquized, "should my good Confederate friends, dacent boys, every mother's son of them, starve and go half-shod with niver a gun or bullet to shoot the inimy that's shooting at them, when the stores in Memphis are running over with what they lack and haven't got?"

After this Hibernianism, Mrs. O'Flaherty set to work in earnest. Into her counsel she took some friends – all brave-spirited and true as steel to the boys in gray. Each became a conspirator and gladly followed her leadership. By the purchase of small lots of supplies in various quarters of the city, they gathered quite a store of clothing, cavalry boots, guns, ammunition, etc., and secreted them in the stables and funeral parlors of which O'Flaherty was the director. All things being in train, a member of the O'Flaherty clan – Mrs. O'Flaherty herself

– was reported ill and later worse, anon dead! A mortuary ad in the daily papers gave due notice of decease and then there was a gathering of sorrowing friends to "wake" the dead O'Flaherty. The next afternoon, an elaborate funeral in keeping with the ancient blood and dignity of an Irish family descended from Irish kings having already been decreed, a long line of carriages, driven by men with faces black as their funeral garb, drew up in front of the overflowing parlors. A heavy, ornate casket was laboriously lifted and borne by six solemn-visaged pall-bearers to a stately hearse, swept at its four corners by ebony plumes to enhance the dismal pomp. Drawn by a span of powerful black horses it led the long, mournful procession that left the mortuary parlors. Slowly, and with evidences of deepest grief, it traversed the streets. Occasionally, a shrill peculiarly weird cry, the Celtic "keening" or lamentation over their dead, broke upon the air and drew the gaping, wonder-eyed idlers to the street corners. Bound for Elmwood Cemetery, a mile off, the solemn train took the same road made famous by the wild, rebel yells and mad dash of Forrest's cavalry raid.

Passing into the cemetery by the much-frequented front entrance, the procession, slowly and decorously, as though not to disturb the deep quiet brooding over the city of the dead, wended its way through the central avenue in the direction of an old, rarely used exit on the opposite side. This exit opened upon a road that, shaded by dense woods, went down to the narrow stream called by the Indians from its refreshing coolness "Nonconnah" (cold water). As the cortege neared this gate, signs of uneasiness began to appear. The hearse bearing the defunct O'Flaherty swayed from side to side. Suddenly, as if the dark forest in front filled them with fear, the noble span of black horses neighed, kicked, reared in affright, pitched forward, then broke from the control of their driver and madly dashed through the gate, down the road, overturning hearse and pitching the casket as if it had been a cockleshell into a clump of shrubbery that grew close by the wayside. At once a stampede followed. As each carriage rolled through the gate, it was as if a grisly phantom beckoned it to doom. The horses, seized with a panic, became utterly unmanageable. In turn they, too, pitched forward, bolted and galloped wildly down the long country road, faster and faster, turning the soft summer stillness into pandemonium with the clatter of their hoofs, and dropping the mourners by the roadside in bushes, ditches, dust and dirt, right and left like so many shelled peas. Nothing could halt the runaway caravan as it frantically tore along making for the distant Nonconnah stream. Only a plunge in its cold waters could exorcise the mad demon of the wood that goaded them to frenzy. Fortunately this wild Gilpin race went by a way back of the Federal guard house, built a mile from its banks, else the "sleeping dogs of war" might have waked, and then it would have gone ill with the O'Flaherty clan.

Wearily picking themselves up from where they had been dumped, still doubtful whether they were on heads or heels, the battered, bruised, limping occupants of the funeral coaches implored each passer-by they chanced to meet in the fast-gathering twilight, to capture their runaway horses and drive them back to the city. Apparently the wave of a magic wand had made their drivers disappear in the grayish-green shadows of the woods, or along the banks of Nonconnah stream. These mourners coming out of the city might have simulated lamentation and deep anguish of spirit, certainly all was genuine on their return.

It was a ludicrous ending to a most successful bit of mummery planned and practiced in the camp of the enemy. The initiated knew that the ponderous casket was innocent mortality, but a receptacle for guns, powder, etc.; that it was skillfully thrown off at a spot agreed upon, to be eagerly seized and plundered by Forrest's bold scouts lying in wait; that many of the mourners threw articles secreted upon their persons into the shrubbery – all so swiftly done in the confusion and uproar of the moment that the most unfriendly eye, had there been one, could not detect them. The drivers were all daring Confederates, who rode after Forrest. Smuggled into the city for the occasion, with faces well blackened, they were at once taken into service by the wild Irishman, O'Flaherty. What a knowing, gleeful twinkle of the eye was his, as he thought of the cunning stampede these bold riders would engineer along the road they had made famous by their early morning raid!

We are glad for the sake of holy things that the priest, bell, book and candle were omitted in this farcical funeral. Although it was well understood among the participants and Southern sympathizers generally that the sturdy, humorous dame was not the defunct in the ghostly mummery exploited as "her funeral," the episode is yet spoken of by the survivors of that day as "Mrs. O'Flaherty's Funeral."

CHAPTER SEVENTEEN

☆ ☆ ☆ ☆

An Incident of the Reconstruction

The State in which our story takes place is Mississippi. To be exact at Wakefield Landing, in Adams County, that looks across the great dividing river upon the parish of Concordia, in its sister Commonwealth, Louisiana. The year was 1873, one of the fatal years in that tragic period of Southern history after the Civil War, known as the "Reconstruction. " It was a time when the negroes, drunk with the new wine of their lately acquired freedom, had abandoned labor in the cane and cotton fields and once more fell to the primitive condition of savagery. Their chief rendezvous was an islet – a spot of greenery known as The Island in Old River, a former channel of the restless, ever-changing Mississippi River. Here they congregated by hundreds and from this place, in prowling bands, roamed the country around, to rob, burn and murder. It was in this turbulent time in early spring that the river, swollen by waters received from its great tributaries above, was becoming an angry flood against its barrier levees. The air was filled with fears of an approaching crevasse, and of wild reports of depredations and crimes committed by the blacks.

Fertile, by reason of rich alluvial deposits, the section of Adams County bordering on the river was largely given to the cultivation of cotton. The plantations being large were miles apart and their crops of cotton, when grown to maturity, effectually concealed the residence of one planter from his neighbor. With neighbors, however, one was not over-burdened, as there were only three houses in sight of Wakefield Landing.

The plantation of Doctor Thurman – an ex-Confederate soldier, a practicing physician and an experimental chemist – was a short distance from the landing with only a broad country road between the house and river. On a certain day, there was great excitement at Wakefield, caused by an influx of the wives of planters with their children. These, greatly alarmed by the threats of the negroes, came to the landing to take a boat for Natchez, thirty-five miles distant, where they would be assured of protection. Strange to say, these women were not accompanied by their husbands – all had suddenly disappeared from home. It was soon decided that the Doctor must go to Natchez for troops with which to quell the negroes. His wife courageously decided to remain behind. Though young in years, she was a fearless heroine of the Sixties and was unwilling to leave their home to be destroyed.

That night she sat alone in the small office of the plantation store. The servants had been dismissed and, after making pallets under the beds for greater security, her helpless, crippled brother-in-law had retired and her three babes had been put to sleep. The night was still, save for the thin, ghostly croaking of frogs from a nearby marsh; the cicadas had long ceased their shrill notes; the whipporwill was silent, and over the broad cotton fields, from the dense forest beyond, the usual lonely hoot of the owl called not to its mate. Only the soft swish of a bat's wings – as, attracted by the light of the lamp, it flew in at an open window – ruffled the silence. A deep hush, as if the night awaited something, sure to happen, had fallen upon the woods, and seemed to deaden the sullen under-tone of the mighty river rolling onward to the Gulf.

Suddenly, the loud report of a pistol coming from the road in the front broke the brooding quiet. Darkness swallowed the sinister echoes and all again was still. At the first shock of the report, Mrs. Thurman sprang from her seat and, with the steady nerves of a woman who had been tried on critical occasions, walked to the door. The hour, the darkness, her lonely condition might well have excused a flutter of nervousness at so unusual an occur-rence – coming when public feeling was so deeply stirred. The door, usually secured by a wooden button was open, but she did not close it. Raising her voice to a pitch from which it could be thrown to a distance, she cried in clear, even tones: "If that nonsense of firing pistols around my house at this hour of the night is not stopped, I will set off the magazine. That will bring the Ku Klux and you well know what that means." It was well that this threat of firing the magazine was not put to the proof for, apart from the rifle called by the plantation hands "Shoot-all-day," the only weapon in the house was a small pistol. Listening intently for the effect of her brave words, she heard stealthy steps as of a number of men slinking around the corner of the yard and retreating through the woods. Their way was down a long country road that led to the Island, three miles off, in a curve of the Mississippi river.

As the sound of steps lost itself in the woods, Mrs. Thurman, with a look upon her face that told of desperate resolve, turned to the store. Against the wall, back of the counter, were ranged four barrels of liquor – one of alcohol for experiments in the laboratory, another of brandy, one of cordial and one of whiskey for use on the plantation. To these she quickly stepped and deftly removed the bung of each. Conscious that the negroes for miles around knew of the liquor in the storehouse, also that it would be their first demand should they return for attack, she was resolved, as it was a matter of kill or be killed, that their first drink should be their last. Serenely, by the light of her lamp, with a hand that trembled not, cool as Judith when about to cut off the head of Holofernes, she went about her work preparing for the worst. From a jar in the laboratory, she selected four lumps of arsenic, each about the size of a small marble, and placed the deadly drug by the open bung of each of the four barrels. It was strange to see a woman young, tender, refined who could prepare a death-dealing dose to slaughter by the wholesale; but her three babes soundly asleep in the next room, helpless and unconscious of peril, was her only thought. Between them and midnight butchery – under God who "taught her hands to war" – was only her puny arm to save both herself and them.

If there were any spies lurking around the house watching her movements, they should see she was not afraid. Entering her bedroom, to give herself an appearance of ease, she picked up some sewing, but, at the same moment, unconsciously glanced at the lowered window.

Pressed against the pane of glass, she saw the hideous face of her negro washerwoman, Barbara, peering into the room; and heard her frightened voice exclaiming: "For Gawd's sake, Miss, do open de door and let me in. Dey say de Ku Kluxes is out to-night, and I'se scairt to death."

Mrs. Thurman had too much at stake to be opening her doors at midnight to admit a negro woman who might be an emissary of the prowling, murderous, savage negro horde of the Island. Too gentle of heart to deny sympathy where she could not give help, she rapped on the window and called out: "Go at once to the quarters, Barbara, and if you are all quiet and well-behaved, I will see that you are protected from the Ku Klux should they come." With a half-choked moan of fear and the cry: "Oh, Gawd! dere comes de Ku Kluxes," the negroes threw up her arms and vanished. In the thick darkness, Mrs. Thurman saw nothing, but it flashed upon her like an illumination that the singular disappearance of the planters was explained – they were members of the Ku Klux Klan, suddenly called out. In those days, a man's oath to the Order allowed him not to tell the secret even to the wife of his bosom. Not until years after the Klan was dissolved did many find it out.

Mrs. Thurman was now assured that a band of the remarkable organization, formed for the purpose of keeping the negro and carpet-bagger element in order, could not be far distant. By their sudden, mysterious appearances after nightfall, apparently from nowhere, the noiseless tread of their horses' muffled feet, fierce grips, ghostly utterances, but above all by their swift, judicial punishment for crimes committed, they kept the half-savage, excitable freedmen from making of the South a second St.

Domingo or Hayti.

Mrs. Thurman turned from the window in peace to await the dawn. The peril had passed, her vigil ended. Her heart bounded with joy, for, with the Klan as guardian of peace and order abroad, she knew that her home and babes were in safety. The next day Doctor Thurman arrived with troops from Natchez, but the negroes had left the Island and, with rapine, fire and slaughter attendant upon their steps, had gone in the direction of Fort Adams, twelve miles distant.

CHAPTER EIGHTEEN

☆　☆　☆　☆

Freedom's Shriek

In the piney woods Parish of St. Helena, La., one morning in the summer of 1865, shortly after the Confederate nation had been buried at Appomattox, a horsemen rode out from the little city of Greensburg and ambled along the dusty country road. He seemed uncertain as to his route, and his military uniform of blue showed plainly that he was a stranger in a strange land. Pausing in front of a two-storied dwelling as if in doubt, he finally opened a gate and leisurely rode through the Staump – an inclosure that served as a barrier to the house-yard beyond. There was an impatience at the sultry heat and a decided business air about the stranger that prevented, while curiously glancing around, his taking in the beauty of the blossomy hedges and their perfume floating in the air. Reining up his horse, he secured it to a post and advanced to meet Mr. C., whose residence he was about to enter.

The Southern planter received his unknown visitor with that habit of courteous hospitality which, for generations, had been handed down in his family as a custom of the country. Invited to enter and be seated, the gentleman in blue briefly informed Mr. C. as to his mission – that he had been sent by his superior of the Freedman's Bureau from a branch established at Baton Rouge, to read to the negroes on his place the Emancipation Proclamation of the late President of the United States. This official declaration of their political status as freedmen he desired to acquaint them with, without delay. Would Mr. C. call them together to hear the document read? The request, though courteously put, was a veiled command. Mr. C., recognizing his impotence to disregard it, at once signified acquiescence and rose to give the necessary order.

To the near-by quarters and over the broad fields, the plantation bell sent a sharp, quick summons. The negroes well understood the language of that bell. Imperatively, it meant prompt obedience to its call. The field-hand quickly unbuckling his mule, mounted and rode to the house, leaving the plough in the furrow; those who had not finished their tin buckets of dinner under the solitary tree left in the cotton field, jumped to their feet and with food in hand, munched as they ran; and women from the quarters, with babies in arms and pickaninnies clinging to their skirts, joined the swelling throng of blacks that came in answer to that imperious, far-reaching, yet musical, jangle of bell.

There was something portentous in the air. All felt it; what could it mean? "Dat bell never talk dat way befo," they assured each other as they crowded through the gate into the backyard. The mystery was more exciting even than Christmas, the Fourth of July, or a funeral, or wedding at the quarters – the festivals and days that usually stirred the quiet pool of their simple, uneventful lives.

At last, they were all gathered, a dark, motley, questioning throng looking up with wondering eyes at the occupants of the gallery, while soliloquizing under their breath: "Yes, dar is Marster and ole Miss, and de chilluns and de young English lady what saved Pomp when de Yanks was raidin' de place; but who am dat soldier-man lookin' so piert, and wid his hand wropped round a big sheet of paper?"

The Government official without more ado, and intent only on getting through with his business, advanced to the edge of the gallery. Placing one hand on the balustrade, in the other he held the Emancipation Proclamation, and, while watching with curiosity the dark faces below to see its effect, read with emphasis the fatal words which assumed to place the dull, ignorant, semi-barbarous slaves of a Southern plantation upon a plane of social equality with that of their master – one who was not only "the heir of all the ages" in point of culture, but whose birth was often of the proudest! Stripped of its legal verbiage and rhetorical varnish, the pith and core of Abraham Lincoln's published ordinance which concerned the negroes recited that "...henceforth, throughout Louisiana, all persons held as slaves shall be free... the military and naval authorities shall recognize and maintain the freedom of said persons... and they are recommended to labor faithfully for reasonable wages." Such is a fragment of the document that, in the words of Earl Russell, had "applied to the States where Government held no power, and did not where it was supreme."

The negroes gaped and stared – about as wise when the reader ended as when he began. In a dazed way they looked at each other, feeling that some matter vitally affecting themselves had occurred, but helpless to trace it out. Had the skies fallen and scattered rainbows? In this sudden breaking loose of Freedom it seemed as though the instincts of motherhood had gone astray, for a baby wriggled from its unheeding mother's arms and sprawling upon the ground, she was content to let it lie in the hot sun like a small black turtle. At this moment, out on the fringe of the circle of newly made freedmen, a ripple of talk in undertone broke the dead pause succeeding the change of old things into new. A tall, black woman wearing a man's trousers under her short cotton skirts, with the air of an African chieftainess, raised her hand. She had caught the words "Lincoln" and "free" – the only words that, in the long paper just read had for her any meaning. Haltingly, circuitously, her memory groped after an incident of the past years, in which an Abolitionist emissary probably was the hero. Turning to the bewildered crowd in the rear, she explained with a vigor that set her bandanna "cornus" quivering: "Yassum, dese eyes done seen dat very man he talk about – de onliest man what could set us free. I seed him in a red flannel shirt and he had on raggedty breeches, and he tole me pintedly his name was Marse Linkum and dat he was comin' to set us free and give us a pacel o' land."

Here another voice added his quota of information: "Yes, Mr. Lincollom, dats a bery good name. I hearn of it in a newspaper one of dem raidin' gen'mens lef, when dey rode outer de front gate." "Sunlight never shined in my cabin door befo' dis day dat tells me I is free," mumbled the carriage driver. "Dat's a bery perlite gen'man. He says we cullud fokes is as free as Marster, and we is got to be paid for our work, too. Lord, Lord, is I a-dreamin'? But what is us gwine to do for somethin' to eat?"

Here into this rosy glamour of freedom, the shovel and hoe laid down, and unrolling before their eyes a bright vista of long days lolling in the warm sunshine, doing nothing but what was prompted by the moment's whim, suddenly obtruded the prosaic, severely practical question of meat and bread. It was a sibilant note that would not down.

Poor black dupes! Until that day, what a kindly bond had existed between themselves and Master! For the first time since their creation was now stamped upon their plastic, childish minds, the dear falsehood of equality – that henceforth, through act of law, they would be equal to the all-conquering, enlightened, ever-dominant Caucasian race! That specious lie caught their childish fancy – eagerly they seized and hugged it closely. To the negro, "Marster" was the synonym for all visible good, and to hear a wonderful story read that made them "gentmans," same as Marster, was as if they were under a spell of necromancy.

In the tree-branches above, a mocking-bird began its strange, sweet medley of song that was confusing, and the scent of the Cherokee roses distilled by the hot sun subtly mixed with this astonishing news of freedom, so that like a potent essence it crept to the brain. The crowd wavered in the bright sunlight. Old and young they had always moved to orders and they had not been told to go away. The reading was over, they were uncertain what to do. If it was true that they were free, then they wouldn't go to the corn and cotton fields in that blazing sun, but lie down in the green grass and go to sleep, or go fishing when it was cooler, or go visiting and find out if slave days were sure enough over.

Into this doubt and indecision, rang out the voice of Mr. C., clearly and incisively. Coming to the edge of the gallery so that all could see and hear him, he cried "Halt!" Uncertaintly vanished at that well-known voice. Like soldiers at the word of command, instantly they were "at attention."

"Men and women," he cried. "you have just heard what this gentleman has read to you, that you are all free from the oldest hand to the last baby born on the place, just as free as he is, as I am, as the President at Washington. But he has told you that you have to work, get pay for it, take care of yourselves and behave. You have heard all this. Now listen to what I have to say."

"You all know that I have been a kind Master, as my farther was before me. I have fed, clothed, sheltered and cared for you. In return you have worked. Now any one who wants to leave the old plantation and work elsewhere can do so, as soon as he gets ready. Whoever stays with me will get honest pay for his work. And now I want to tell you something more. About this work there is to be no shirking. You have got to take orders from me, and there is to be no more foolishness in the future about your working, than there has been in the past. On this place I am always Master, yet always your friend. Now go to your work and to the quarters."

"Yes Marster; sure enough, Marster; 'deed you are right, Marster," broke in cheery tone from the sable crowd as with an obedience that was instinctive, the negroes briskly moved from the yard. The mirage of "do nothing all day long" faded into nothingness; all desire for a siesta in the soft, green grass under a pine tree, or the attractions of the fish pond or bayou had melted away under the cool, crisp commands of the master. Again the

plantation bell rang. Its voice was the symbol of authority. Like the great iron Roland – liberty-loving bell of
Ghent – it had called men and women to freedom. But the
free burghers of Ghent had free souls that resisted servi-
tude. Here, to the brazen clang of the bell, slaves both in
mind and body had responded. Forthwith the plowman
returned to his forsaken furrow, still doubtful if he were
not walking in his sleep, or dreaming; the cotton hand
shouldered his hoe and hurried to make up for lost time.
To their elemental, unawakened intelligence, liberty
meant only such as the wild animals of the woods knew
– an existence rounded by eating, sleeping and idling.

The agent of the Freedmen's Bureau, crumpling
his proclamation in pocket passed a handkerchief over his
heated brow. He loved not the fierce heat of a Louisiana
sun and the day's work had been strenuous. His lip curled
contemptuously as he followed with his eyes the men and
women obediently filing out to the fields. "Cattle," was
the word that escaped him. His duty to his superior had
ended, and the consequences of his morning's work were
for others to shoulder. Affably taking leave of Mr. C., he
rode back to Greensburg scarcely vouchsafing a thought
– at the most one of indifference – to the momentous
problem that day given to the planter to work out.

The End

Made in the USA
Monee, IL
07 July 2026